The Mosaic Tile Co...

The Mosaic Tile Company

History and Products,
1894–1967

LARISA HARPER

McFarland & Company, Inc., Publishers

Jefferson, North Carolina

*All photographs are by the author
unless otherwise noted.*

ISBN (print) 978-1-4766-8795-7
ISBN (ebook) 978-1-4766-4561-2

LIBRARY OF CONGRESS AND BRITISH LIBRARY
CATALOGUING DATA ARE AVAILABLE

Brick façade of Mosaic Tile Company (author's photograph)

Printed in the United States of America

*McFarland & Company, Inc., Publishers
Box 611, Jefferson, North Carolina 28640
www.mcfarlandpub.com*

In loving memory of my father
whom we lost far too soon:
Richard W. Higdon

In honor of my mother for her love and support—
we love you more: Janette E. Higdon

Table of Contents

Acknowledgments

This resource was made possible with the help, support, knowledge, and enthusiasm of multiple people in my life—new friends and old, family, and fellow collectors. Special thanks and acknowledgment to the following people for being an important part of this book and, hopefully, future books.

New Friends
David M. Taylor, Curator, Muskingum County History
Jerry Thompson, Zane Grey and National Road Museum
Mayor Donald L. Mason, City of Zanesville
Rick Sabine, Secrest Auditorium
Jerri Elson, Muskingum Residentials, Inc.
Pastor Mark Combs and W. Norman Shade, St. John's Lutheran Church
Joe Morrison, Facebook's Muskingum County History/Photos/Memories
James M. Campsey, Jr., Clossman Unique Market
Paul Emory, artist and downtown Zanesville business owner
Jeffrey Snyder, Olde Towne Antique Mall
Jennifer Martin, Quality Care Partners
Bruce C. Dunzweiler, relative of Byron Schrider (designer for Mosaic Tile Company)
Gary Allen, Facebook's Zanesville Video History Group and Zane's Trace Commemoration
Jeff Koehler, Koehler Auctions
Dave Briggs, Koehler Auctions
Pastor Tara Mitchell, Central Presbyterian Church
Jay Bennett, formerly of City of Zanesville
Sheila Menzies, Tile Heritage Foundation
Rick Buck, Zane's Trace Commemoration

Special Friends
Dr. Terry and Paul Herman
Pam Kirst and Mark Zanghi
Heather Sands
Heather Shepherd
Dr. Elizabeth Kline
Tracey Tonnous
Wendy Koile
Dr. Rebecca and Richard Watts

Karin Kauffmann Pangels and Henning Pangels

Erika Pennachio

Tara Adornetto

Anne Littick Hoffer

Faith United Methodist family: Pastor Joy Wigal, Jim and Barb Tignor, Marsha Kelly, Gail McGreevy, Teresa Felton, Susie Dunlap, Betty Howard, Cindy and Nick Howard, and many others who make Sundays, and all days, special.

Colleagues: Patty Klein, Becky Harr, Dr. Brenda Haas, Dr. Stephanie Davidson, Charles See, Michelle Chavanne, Carlos King I, Sara Molski, Drew Sevel, Dr. Krista Maxson, Laura Padgett, Mitzi Dunn, Wendy Casterline

Especially my family

My husband, Aaron; son, A.J., daughters, Cassie and Jordee

Janette Higdon, mother

Paul Harper, father-in-law

My siblings and their families: David & Gaylin Higdon, Pam & Jabie Conrad, Shelly Higdon, Janine and Wayne King, Rick and Jodi Higdon, Barb and Keith Wolfe, Julie and Dan Ardrey, and Todd and Kathy Higdon, and all of our nieces and nephews, great-nieces and great-nephews. Special thanks to Barb for her awesome Mosaic Tile finding skills and to Gaylin for her love of collecting.

In special memory of my father, Richard Higdon, and my mother-in-law, Carol Harper

For those of you who have helped, and I have omitted your name, please know it is an unintentional oversight. I am incredibly grateful, and I owe you a drink.

Preface

"Mom, I think you have a problem." I struggled to understand what I had heard my daughter say. "An addiction," she added. Her words were familiar to me, but I could not comprehend entirely. We had been wandering around an antique store on the hunt for treasures. She went for the final emphasis. "You have too many tiles." Wait, what?

I slowly lowered the dusty tile I was holding to a sales shelf. I had just found it on the floor of the vendor's booth. I had already checked the back of the tile and had found the recognizable logo of the Mosaic Tile Company—a raised elongated horizontal racetrack-shaped oval with the capital letters, MOSAIC, within. These items had been made by turn of the 20th century Zanesville citizens—beloved grandparents and parents of the people I have met in antique stores, museums, and on social media pages—people who love the history of the company and the area.

I did not see my collection of tiles as a problem. To me, it was an act of protection. My quest to protect these Mosaic tiles had been instilled in me because my parents, my eight siblings, and I lived in a house near Zanesville, Ohio, which had been decorated with thousands of tiles. I am not exaggerating—thousands! Several of the walls, ceilings, and floors were covered with monochromatic color schemes of blue, green, brown, yellow, red, and golden tiles. Instead of wallpaper and paint, someone had used the tiles for the interior design.

While growing up, the tiles were normal décor to me. These were just part of the house; I barely noticed them until the occasional tile fell to the floor. I do not remember exactly when Mom shared "the story" with me. The story made these tiles more personal to me. The story brought a big world down to a small size.

The characters of the story were a real-life family in 1950, Otto and Margaret Kauffman and their children, Karin (15 years old), Kristin (13), Otto IV (11) and Ulrich (7), who had moved to Zanesville after a harrowing escape from eastern Germany after World War II. After emigrating to the U.S., Otto landed a job at the Mosaic Tile Company as the ceramic engineer. They bought a home about five miles south of the company's headquarters. This real estate bounty was a three-story house with a full basement; it had once been a farm's barn. Over a five-year period, Otto spent time with his family decorating the home with Mosaic's tiles in multiple colors and shapes.

The story transitioned in 1956 when the Kauffmann family moved again for a new employment opportunity in Canada. Along came the Higdon family: Richard, father; Janette, mother; and their four children, David (7 years old), Pamela (5 years old), Michele (2 years old), Janine (1 years old), and a fifth child, Rick, was on his way. My parents raised a total of nine children in that house (including Barbara, Julie, Todd, and Larisa) and, over the decades, memories have intertwined with the tiles even as the structure of the home began to need repairs. In present day, my husband and I have been working to restore the home and its tiles.

My appreciation for the Mosaic Tile Company began as a child surrounded by the tile and now as an adult as a collector, protector, and chronicler of the history and the products of the company. I do not claim to have expertise in the field of ceramics or art pottery. My passion is simply to tell the story of this company in order to fill a gap in the anthology of the ceramics industry. Many details about the history of the industry, the production of tiles and ceramic figures, and the science associated with the creation of these pieces are gleaned from attributed resources. There are likely many products from the Mosaic Tile Company that are not included in this book because of lack of trade-marking or because they were not discovered by me during my research. What we learn from this point onward may warrant another book to include the new treasures along with the stories associated with the families of this company.

I hope that you enjoy reading this book as much as I have enjoyed collecting and learning from the Mosaic Tile Company.

1

The Founding of Zanesville, Ohio

Three community members working together to create a new company in the burgeoning ceramic industry in the late 1800s was reminiscent of the three primary founders exploring and creating the new city of Zanesville, Ohio, in the late 1700s. The story of the three ceramic leaders, Karl Langenbeck, Herman Mueller, and William Shinnick, followed almost 100 years after the western trek of the founding fathers, Ebenezer Zane, John McIntire, and Dr. Increase Mathews, and the beginnings of a city in the brand new state of Ohio as a doorway to new trails to the west.

A federally commissioned path to the west featured Colonel Ebenezer Zane blazing his "Zane's Trace," from the city of Wheeling, then part of Virginia, to Limestone, in Kentucky, in the late 1790s. This trail would lead to new opportunities, new land for veterans of the Revolutionary War, and new fertile property for farming in the nation. Upon the end of this war, the new country of the United States found itself without money to compensate its soldiers. Many soldiers returned to their homes after suffering from hunger, wounds, and fear and found that their families also had suffered greatly financially. The U.S. Congress sought ways to repay the soldiers without cash.[1] Instead, the government gave land grants, for example in the future state of Ohio, known as the Northwest Territory at that time. The land, in what is now known as the southern half of Ohio, was the area granted by Congress to many soldiers, including Colonel Ebenezer Zane.[2]

Zane had written to Congress to suggest an exchange: Zane would construct a road and ferry services along the path from his home in Wheeling in the state of Virginia to Limestone (now Maysville) in Kentucky as a trade for consolidating his land grants together, when usually these were not contiguous.[3] Congress agreed to Zane's proposal and, eventually, Zane's Trace led the travelers into the Northwest Territory through lands that crossed the Muskingum, Hocking (originally named Hock-hocking), and Scioto Rivers.[4]

Zane's group headed westward in 1796 and included ferrymen Henry Crooks and William McCullough (sometimes spelled McColloch); Zane's son-in-law, John McIntire; and Zane's brother, Jonathan.[5] Part of his deal with Congress was that Zane had to cover his own expenses, and he had to establish ferry services at the river crossings.

Once the trail had been finished and Zane's land had been consolidated, in 1799, Zane transferred the land to McIntire and Jonathan Zane as compensation for their work on the trail and charged the men $100, which would be just over $2,000 in 2020.[6] McIntire and McCullough built homes near the river: McCullough's was near his ferry service at the end of what became Main Street and McIntire's home was near today's Market Street. McCullough's home soon also became the landing point of postal mail traveling north on the Muskingum River from the previously established city of Marietta. With that natural association, McCullough also began serving as the city's first postmaster in 1801.[7] (Various sources cite different dates for the founding of Zanesville. The dates of 1797, 1799, and 1801 are most common. Most Zanesville official city citations use 1797 as the founding date.[8])

Initially, McIntire named the city Westbourne, but when the postal service began its regular deliveries to the area, in about 1801, another individual associated with the postal service determined that this town had been part of Zane's trace and a better name for the city would be Zanesville.[9] Some historical accounts also indicated that the town was named Zanefield or Zanetown for a time, but Zanesville won out.[10]

McIntire and Jonathan Zane divided Ebenezer Zane's land, with McIntire keeping the area now known as downtown Zanesville.[11] McIntire's home, a double-log cabin, built at the southwest corner of Market and Second Streets, had plenty of room for his family and for travelers who were on their way to new lands and opportunities.[12] This became the first inn and it served as a stopping point for the people who were crossing the Muskingum River because McIntire would purposely invite those travelers to lodge at his inn.[13] While staying, McIntire would use his best sales pitch to convince those who were talented in trades to purchase land lots in Zanesville and to add their skills to the growing city's population. Within a few years and with McCullough's help, McIntire had laid out the streets of Zanesville by clearing trees and brush and outlining the streets.[14]

Several acres of land west of the Muskingum River, across from the original Zanesville area, became available for purchase and were to be sold in auction in 1801. Several individuals were interested in the land for development. McIntire vied for the property along with his competitor Dr. Increase Mathews. Mathews had traveled to the Ohio Country in 1800 to visit his uncle, General Rufus Putnam, who had gained fame for settling Marietta and inspiring other pioneers to settle in the west.[15] Mathews arrived in Zanesville in 1801 with his wife and daughter. He established himself as the Zanesville area's first doctor, and within months added landowner as one of his roles.

As both McIntire and Mathews traveled separately toward Marietta for the land auction, they came upon each other as they rode on horses. They continued together to Marietta without telling the other the purpose of their travel.[16] When they arrived in Marietta, the travelers went separate ways with Mathews traveling to the home of his uncle, General Rufus Putnam. Putnam and Mathews' cousin Levi Whipple pooled their funds for the auction (with Putnam being the primary funding source). The next day, McIntire and Mathews realized that they had traveled together for the same auction for the land west of the Muskingum River. Mathews ended up outbidding McIntire with an offer of $4.25 an acre compared to McIntire's losing bid of $4.[17]

Dr. Mathews was not only a physician but an entrepreneur. His purchase of the property was based on his uncle's advice that the future in the United States would be filled with travelers seeking new adventures and livelihoods in the Northwest Territory.[18] Since Zanesville was growing, Mathews considered building along the Muskingum River across from Zanesville as an opportunity to bring great advantages for tradespeople and their families. While his physician work was part of his life, he concentrated in those early years on this new land named Springfield by plotting and selling the land. In 1805, Dr. Mathews joined the new homebuilders by constructing a one-story "sandstone house on his land at what is now the corner of Washington Street and Woodlawn Avenue."[19]

Dr. Mathews had lived to see Springfield, which was re-named Putnam after McIntire's uncle General Putnam in 1814, become a busy town with a population of 1,500 by the time of his death in 1856.[20] His dedication and entrepreneurship in building Putnam was remarkably similar to McIntire's work for Zanesville across the river. His home, now a museum, is part of the Muskingum County History, the area's historical society.

Even in defeat in acquiring the land west of the river, McIntire continued to find ways to make Zanesville sustainable, if not profitable. For instance, he wanted the burgeoning government of Ohio to name Zanesville as the state capital. At the time, the state's seat of government was in Chillicothe, but an official capital had not been decided.[21] Being named a state capital offered fortune such as funds for establishing social and civic services, roads, canals, bridges, and dams along the rivers in addition to food and lodging for legislators and visitors and basic services as print shops, tax offices, and business supplies.[22]

In 1809, Zanesville leaders constructed a 5,000 square foot brick building for their version of a statehouse. McIntire took advantage of his growing wealth to offer the brick building at no cost to the state government. Across the river, Putnam leaders decided

Dr. Increase Mathews' home on Woodlawn Avenue, built in 1805.

The Stone Academy on Jefferson Street.

to compete for the statehouse honor as well. Dr. Mathews, Ebenezer Buckingham, Levi Whipple, and Henry Mathews organized and built a large two-story, 3,000 square foot building in 1809, which was eventually named the Stone Academy.[23]

On February 19, 1810, Zanesville was named the temporary state capital for Ohio. While McIntire was hoping that this temporary site would become permanent, influential leaders in the legislature created a committee to name and construct a permanent location within about 40 miles of the center of the state. Nevertheless, the Zanesville brick capital building was used for the work of Ohio's legislature from October 1, 1810, to May 1, 1812.

A unique geographical feature of the area, the confluence of the Muskingum and Licking Rivers, bordered the city of Zanesville just north of McCullough's ferry crossing. These rivers and their subsequent bridges would provide the transportation needed for people and goods of the trades that were being added to the Zanesville area. The unique terrain added to the burgeoning population and held great potential for any industry, and in those years, especially for the ceramic and pottery businesses.

Initially, the ferries, first established by McCullough, were used to cross the low-lying rivers to and from Putnam and Zanesville and other areas near those towns. These ferries were basic transportation consisting of two canoes connected by planks and ropes.[24] The growth of businesses along the rivers prompted city leaders to build a bridge that would take travelers from Zanesville proper to western and northern parts of the

The Y-Bridge postcard, 1832–1900.

The Y-Bridge postcard, 1902–1984.

The Y-Bridge, 1984 to present.

area. While operating in Zanesville, the Ohio General Assembly authorized the building of a toll bridge "from a point opposite of the Main Street of Zanesville to an island at the mouth of the Licking, thence north and south each way across the mouth of the Licking creek."[25] Travelers were charged to help pay for bridge maintenance.

What better kind of bridge could be created than one that would span the confluence of the Muskingum and Licking Rivers? The first of its kind, a "Y" shaped bridge was conceived and, in the fall of 1814, was completed at the foot of Main Street in Zanesville.[26] From Main Street, travelers had two choices. One choice was to venture west and in the middle of the Y-Bridge, the travelers could turn left toward West Main Street, leading

John McIntire gravesite on the grounds of Zanesville City Schools, formerly near the site of the John McIntire Children's home.

westward along the Licking River. The second choice was to head toward the northeast by turning right in the middle of the bridge and traveling Linden Avenue toward what became the McIntire Historic District, northwest of downtown Zanesville.

This first Y-Bridge was a wooden bridge "constructed of wooden trestles and stone with logs and planks bolted to the trestles."[27] This bridge, without any covering, eventually succumbed to the harshness of the Ohio weather and collapsed in 1818. A second Y-Bridge, a partially covered wooden bridge, was built in 1819. When the National Road was built through Zanesville in 1830 and included the Y-Bridge, the traffic load along with a dangerous flood in 1831 weakened the structure.[28] In early 1832, the bridge was condemned. The third Y-Bridge, which was a completely covered wooden bridge, was opened in December 1832 and lasted until 1900.[29] The toll payment was collected until 1868 when county commissioners bought the bridge and ended the toll charges.[30] This third bridge also could not handle the increased traffic with the growing population along with the electric streetcars that had been installed. The fourth Y-Bridge was opened in 1902 and survived even with minor damage from the major 1913 flood until 1983.[31] Finally, the fifth and current Y-Bridge was opened in 1984 and was made of concrete and steel.[32] It was designed to resemble the 1902 bridge in response to historic preservation authorities.[33]

Zanesville's founder, McIntire, who lived until 1815, saw the opening of the first Y-Bridge and the beginning of the National Road. During his lifetime, he saw the area's population grow to over 1,000 people within 18 years.[34] He also established the Zanesville Canal and Manufacturing Company to capitalize on future dam and canal construction.[35] Although the Zanesville Canal and Manufacturing Company was not especially lucrative during his lifetime, the company continued and added the work of overseeing McIntire's estate.[36] The funds bequeathed by McIntire have supported Zanesville area children and education among other causes and is still strong.[37]

The foundations laid by Ebenezer Zane, John McIntire, and Dr. Increase Mathews with the blazing of the Trace, Zanesville, and the founding Putnam, have been the solid rock on which the Zanesville area began its historical pioneering in a land of the unknown. These three established the exciting future for industrious men and women in southeastern Ohio for the next two hundred years.

2

Establishing the Pottery
Industry in Southeastern Ohio

Given the opportunities of new towns and growing populations, the door to the western territories was wide open to travel along the newly created Zane's Trace road, navigable rivers, the Y-Bridge, and the National Road. With the western trek of pioneers into the newly borne state of Ohio, many stopped along these roadways and waterways in the growing towns of Zanesville and Putnam. These pioneer families spread out within the area to claim or buy lands and began the work of establishing farms and businesses. With Zanesville as its county seat, Muskingum County, named in 1804, began bustling with industry as the settlers brought their talents from the eastern cities and towns. These townspeople likely also learned from area Indigenous Americans how to survive in this unchartered region.

Ohio Clay

What drew entrepreneurs to the area and what product was so naturally plentiful to allow these groups to flourish? "An abundant supply of … clay resources that are ideally suited as raw material for production of high-quality ceramic products."[1] This natural resource has been described as a "highly prized material when touched by the artist and moulded into a thing of beauty."[2] In 1838, Caleb Atwater predicted great geological opportunities for those who used the clay within Muskingum and Perry Counties (the county just south of Muskingum), "a white clay is found, in abundance, suitable for pots and crucibles … it stands the heat very well … it will one day, be used extensively, in the manufacture of … earthernwares."[3] Additionally, Everhart and Graham reported that early mining and use of local clay "found it good in two varieties, one burning red, and the other buff, and as other colors could be made by the desired pigments."[4] This abundance of the red clay contributed to the brick-making industry in the area: "Pressed brick manufacture began in Zanesville in 1875 and soon grew into a thriving industry. By 1886, the Zanesville area was regarded as producing some of the finest ornamental and enameled brick in the country."[5] In order to assist with clarity, buff clay is a very natural earthy color with content of "materials sufficiently high in iron to fire buff rather than white in color."[6] The reddish color of red clay is made up of a "large percentage of iron oxide, and there are many variations of this natural color to be found in tiles ranging from deep reddish browns to softer and paler oranges and pinks."[7] White clay is a clay with a "minimum amount of contaminants."[8]

According to Ries and Leighton, Indigenous Americans had made clay products and began what is considered one of the "oldest industries" in the United States.[9] Additionally, Europeans who had immigrated to the United States brought with them their own talents in the clay industry. When traveling westward, they found the raw materials needed for quality clay products within the Muskingum County region. According to a report produced for the 1895 Ohio General Assembly, it was confirmed that Muskingum County, "in the vicinity of Zanesville and Roseville," was likely the "original seat of the pottery business."[10]

Area Growth

A perfect storm began to form in the Zanesville area in the late 1800s. First, with the growth of the city by travelers following Zane's Trace, the National Road, and, eventually, the railroad, the area experienced a "population boom that would send the city from 10,000 citizens in 1870 to more than 23,000 by 1900."[11] The railroads also aided travel and growth that were being built across the nation which "crisscrossed the state and connected the Muskingum River cities with markets … [and] industries developed more rapidly."[12] Next, the growth of manufacturing companies of glass, iron, pottery, and tiles were aided by the mechanical inventions of the Industrial Revolution. At the center of this storm, Zanesville, which was buttressed by potteries throughout Muskingum County and the towns of Roseville and Crooksville, became known as "The Clay Capital of the World," "The Pottery belt," "The Clay Corridor," and "The Clay City." Zanesville led the way for the clay industry to serve as a major economic contributor in the newly independent United States and newly established state of Ohio.

Bluebird Potteries

Bluebirds are harbingers of spring in Ohio and were the symbol of the earliest potteries in the western U.S. lands. Bluebird potteries set the foundation for Ohio's growth into leadership of the clay industry. According to James Murphy, who had studied extensively the early establishments of potteries, the "rural bluebird potteries began springing up in the western and southwestern part of the [Muskingum] county as early as 1814."[13] Bluebird potteries may have taken on that name due to the timing of the farmers' creation of products in late winter or early spring when the bluebirds returned to Ohio after their trip south. Another origin of the name is the description of the cobalt blue used as decoration on the products, which was reminiscent of the birds' colorful feathers. Regardless of which folklore to believe, these farming families numbered nearly 200 in Muskingum County between 1850 and 1880.[14]

Farmers in the Ohio region benefited from weather suited for crops from spring through fall, but during the winter months, little farming could be completed. During those cold wintry months, the farmers found themselves using the abundance of clay from the area to create utilitarian clay products that could be used year-round. The farmers usually had the tools needed for working with the clay—machinery and horses to dig and till the soil, to sift and press the clay, and hearths or outdoor ovens to fire the products. They would then, in the spring, take their local clay products to town to trade for other needed supplies. Since cash was in slim supply in the Zanesville and Putnam towns, these stoneware products were nicknamed "Putnam currency" as these items were useful to all and easily traded for other supplies.[15] Some produced enough to load their wares onto boats to send down the Muskingum, Ohio, and Mississippi Rivers toward New Orleans to find new markets and customers.[16]

First Potteries in Area

While many small bluebird potteries were beginning and growing, Samuel Sullivan has the credit for crafting pottery in the Zanesville area around 1808 or 1810 (the date varies among sources).[17] Sullivan, originally from Philadelphia, had a shop located on North Third Street in Zanesville. He produced redware plates, pitchers, and cups using clays he found in the local area. Sullivan was one of those early producers of ceramic products that were loaded on "flatboats and sold down the river as far as New Orleans."[18]

Another early entrepreneur, Solomon Purdy, began a business on what is now known as Putnam Avenue between Jefferson and Madison Streets in 1820.[19] Purdy produced bowls, plates, and dishes of red and yellow ware.[20] The next group of pottery producers, Howson, Hallam, Wheaton, and Tunnicliffe, came from Staffordshire, England, sometime in the 1840s. Some accounts group the four together in the timing of their arrivals, while others have Tunnicliffe arriving eight years after the first three in 1848.[21] These were all specifically associated with Rockingham pieces, which are brown glazed earthenware. There were enough producers of pottery to account for the "largest export of 212,631 pounds of pottery" in 1842.[22]

While other pottery artisans were starting businesses throughout Muskingum County, Frederick H. Hall was the next early pottery player in the Zanesville area. He arrived around 1874 with the financial support of Benedict Fischer of New York. Hall was tasked with experimenting with the clays of the area for tile production. Hall eventually had patented this process of "experimenting with fire clay" which he created in the former Howson and Hallam Pottery building in Zanesville.[23] In 1875, Hall worked with Gilbert Elliott and Benedict Fischer to incorporate the American Encaustic Tiling Company and together they created their first major project of decorative tile for the Muskingum County Courthouse, dedicated in 1877.

While the American Encaustic Tiling Company is known as the first major pottery and tile company in the city of Zanesville, it was not the first in Muskingum County. Sometime in 1872 or 1873, in the small town of Fultonham in the southwestern part of the county, Samuel Weller began his small clay company in a log cabin, where he focused on the practical items of flowerpots, crocks, and bowls. He later moved his company to Zanesville in 1882 as he outgrew his small cabin home and needed more factory space. Weller Pottery eventually grew into one of the largest potteries in the early 1900s.

As noted, dates of incorporation have been blurred over time and some names have been forgotten to history, but what is obvious is the incredible number of entrepreneurs in what became the clay industry in southeastern Ohio. Researchers Murphy and Morton noted that statistics and details are only available for a few years "suggesting inconsistencies on the part of the information gatherers."[24] Further, they found that directories "suffer from gross misspellings, as well as ambiguities regarding exact locations."

Neighboring Towns

In the early days, even with the growth of small towns, citizens were separated and limited to travel via horses. Advances in transportation not only helped people become more mobile, the production and sale of pottery were assisted as modern travel options emerged. The local newspaper reported that street railway service began in 1874.[25] Within another 3 decades, there were more than 65 passenger trains running to and from Zanesville daily by the early 20th century.[26]

The construction of the Cincinnati, Wilmington, and Zanesville Railroad gave residents of Roseville, a town in southern Muskingum County, more options to transport products to Zanesville for shopping and selling in 1856.[27] The improved transportation helped the growth of pottery companies in Roseville. William Lenhart owned the first credited pottery in Roseville on "Potter's Alley" in 1838.[28] Roseville's own documentation indicated that in 1866, nine bluebird potteries were in operation in or near Roseville.[29] William J. Watt is credited with buying land rich with clay and coal in 1886 and founding the Brilliant Stoneware Company. That company was abandoned after a fire in 1897 when Watt purchased the Globe Stoneware Company in nearby Crooksville and re-christened it the Watt Pottery Company. After Watt's death in 1923, the family attempted to keep the company afloat but eventually decided to branch into another direction.

In 1885, J.B. Owens began his life in the pottery business with "a small shop with a kiln and wheel."[30] His successful business grew quickly, and Zanesville leaders encouraged him to move to their city.[31] In approximately 1891, Owens moved his company to the newly organized Brighton district in Zanesville.[32] The company underwent various changes such as adding the manufacturing of art pottery before J.B. Owens sold his company. Owens then began a new opportunity with the manufacture of floor and wall tiles with his Empire Floor and Wall Tile Company in 1914.

The Roseville Pottery Company was incorporated in 1890 in Roseville and focused on "commercial pottery such as stoneware, flowerpots, and cuspidors."[33] The company's growth in less than a decade spurred them to buy the Clark Stoneware factory on Linden Avenue in Zanesville in 1898.[34] The Linden Avenue plant, which Roseville Pottery closed in 1954, was later purchased by the Mosaic Tile Company.

Starting in 1901 by four brothers, the Ransbottom Stoneware Company originated in the small town of Ironspot near Roseville.[35] After various mergers and acquisitions, the Robinson Ransbottom Pottery Company (RRPC) was a staple of the Roseville area with RRPC well-known for its many utilitarian products and, still sought after, pet bowls and saucers.

The McCoy family name became well-known in pottery circles in 1848 with the work of W. Nelson McCoy and his uncle, W.F. McCoy in the Putnam area.[36] Later in 1899, a relative, J.W. McCoy, opened his pottery company in Roseville. Over time, the company grew and bought other companies that came with name changes to Brush-McCoy in 1911 and Brush Pottery Company in 1925. Nelson McCoy began with his work as Nelson McCoy Sanitary and Stoneware Company in 1910 and changed its focus with a name of Nelson McCoy Pottery in 1932. Nelson McCoy Pottery had been sold many times over the years, and it eventually closed in 1990. Art pottery collectors faithfully still seek the products of this company.

Burley Clay Products joined the mix in 1923 with stoneware crocks and jugs, and, by 1933, focused on garden ware and birdbaths in Roseville. In 1996, Burley partnered with Robinson Ransbottom Pottery to continue the manufacturing of Robinson Ransbottom's products. The company proudly shares on its website that it continues as the only stoneware manufacturer in the area. The "lost art" process of jiggering is still used by Burley employees who have learned through years of apprenticeship work how to conduct this hand-worked process.[37] Additionally, Burley artists have continued the long tradition of hand-painting the decoration for their birdbaths, pedestals, and planters.[38]

Located between Roseville and Zanesville was a lesser-known company but still important in the area's history, Gonder Ceramic Arts, Inc. Leaders John D. Peters and Adam Reed had purchased an old factory of the South Zanesville Clay Manufacturing Company in 1897 to produce art pottery.[39] In 1915, local entrepreneur H.S. McClelland bought the Peters' and Reed's plant and started the new Zane Pottery.[40] McClelland retired in 1914 and closed the Zane Pottery. Lawton Gonder, a Zanesville native who had worked throughout the country for multiple pottery and tile companies "signed the deed for the former Zane Pottery and named his new company Gonder Ceramic Arts, Inc." in 1941.[41] Gonder specialized in "higher priced art pottery" for many years and later added ceramic tile until he sold his business in 1957.[42]

Sample collection of Hull Pottery (top row) and Watt Pottery (bottom row).

Samples of McCoy Pottery.

Samples of Robinson-Ransbottom Pottery Company.

Samples of American Encaustic Tiling Company.

Arts and Crafts Movement

With the area's roots in bluebird potteries, the utilitarian usefulness of bowls, crocks, and jars played important roles in frontier families' lives. But as noted, many potteries began with useful products and grew into the more artistic creativeness of ceramic products. This shift coincided with the Art Pottery Movement in the United States which began in the late 1870s. Part of the overall Arts and Crafts Movement, art tile and art pottery began to be a focus of some of the larger pottery companies. According to Grimmer and Konrad, it was "in the Victorian era that ceramic tile flooring first became so prevalent in the U.S. The production of decorative tiles in America began about 1870 and flourished until about 1930."[43] The 1876 Centennial Exhibition in Philadelphia may be credited for the popularity of art tiles in homes, as noted in an art pottery book that "many middle-class and wealthy customers modeled their homes in the latest fashions with art tiles."[44] Further, art pottery was also spotlighted at the 1893 Chicago World's Columbian Exposition; this led into the booming years of the art pottery business at the turn of the 20th century, and Ohio was a leading producer of these items.[45]

3

Mosaic Tile Company Begins: 1894 through World War I

The year 1894 was a year of several milestones: It had been 97 years since the founding of Zanesville, 91 years since the founding of Ohio, 54 years since the end of the first Industrial Revolution, and 29 years since the end of the Civil War. It was also the year of the incorporation of the Mosaic Tile Company in Zanesville, Ohio.

In that year, two employees of the American Encaustic Tiling (AET) Company in Zanesville, Karl Langenbeck and Herman C. Mueller, had decided to begin their own tile company. Opinions on why they left AET vary. Some believed that the two knew they were key players in profit-making for AET, and they wanted a bigger share. Others believed that Langenbeck and Mueller envisioned a new artistic plan for American ceramics, and they needed their own business to support that vision.

Regardless of the reason, the two experienced and educated ceramicists were ready to partner with financial supporters and incorporate the Mosaic Tile Company. Prior to and during Mueller's and Langenbeck's tenures at AET, they were setting themselves apart from others in the industry. Each had traveled a unique path to founding Mosaic, and events along the way brought the team together.

Karl Langenbeck, born in 1861 in Cincinnati, Ohio, was remarkably talented within the field of chemistry, specifically ceramic chemistry. He was a graduate of the College of Pharmacy in Cincinnati in 1882; had studied at the Technische Hochschule in Berlin, Germany and the Polytechnic School in Zurich, Switzerland; and had taken chemistry courses at the University of Cincinnati.[1] A story has been told in many accounts that Langenbeck showed a keen interest in the art of ceramics as early as 12 years old. He had a china-painting set and had been enthralled with painting when a woman who was visiting his mother noticed his interest as well and, as the story goes, she borrowed Langenbeck's paint set until she could get her own. That same woman, Maria Longworth Nichols, later became the founder and owner of Rookwood Pottery in Cincinnati, and Langenbeck, just eleven years after that first meeting, eventually worked there as a chemist, in 1884.[2] After Rookwood, he used his knowledge of ceramic chemistry to help establish the short-lived Avon Pottery Company in 1886 in Cincinnati. From there he ventured to Zanesville to join the AET staff as the chemical engineer in 1890. Langenbeck, known as the first ceramic chemist, used his talents for chemistry to author *The Chemistry of Pottery* in 1895.[3] This book filled a gap in the literature for the profession and became the ultimate textbook for other chemists working in the ceramic industry.[4] The focus of the book included the heating of clays and the importance of the chemical formula of glazes.

Longtime Zanesville historian Norris F. Schneider quoted an unknown source indicating that Langenbeck had "introduced parian vitreous bodies to take the place of the white and light colored tile," and claimed Langenbeck had also "introduced dust inlaid encaustic tile and cones for firing control."[5] Parian vitreous is described as a porcelain that has a higher amount of a mineral that produces a glass-like appearance and is "much smoother than biscuit porcelain."[6] Encaustic tiles include those "in which the ornamental design is formed in the clay itself...."[7]

Herman C. Mueller began his work in the creative arts as a sculptor. His birth in Germany placed him in the center of major contributions for the ceramic industry at that time. Highly educated in his youth, he attended the Preparatory Art School and the Industrial Academy in Nuremberg, Germany, and the Art Academy in Munich. When he ventured to Cincinnati, he began as an artist and sculptor with his own studio. Over time, he held various positions at multiple potteries in the Cincinnati area such as Matt Morgan Art Pottery and Kensington Art Pottery before he left for Indianapolis in 1885. For this, he was commissioned to design the architectural ornaments for the Indiana State Capitol in Indianapolis.[8] His next stop was Zanesville for employment at AET as its modeler in 1887. A modeler is one "who with infinite pains fashions and refashions the plastic clay into preconceived forms of beauty and utility."[9] Wires et al. also complimented Mueller when they indicated that he "possessed in high degree the ability to marry sculpture with tile."[10] At AET Mueller specialized in making relief tiles, on which an image is sculpted and projects outward from the base tile.[11]

Mueller was making news in the industry from both the artistic and technical sides. Michael Sims, prolific author of pottery books and articles, pronounced that the "artistic quality of the [American Encaustic Tiling] Company's tiles" improved greatly when Mueller was employed there.[12] Further, Sims indicated that "Mueller's fireplace surrounds and classical figure panels are among the finest art tiles ever produced."[13] Mueller was credited by multiple sources for improving the artistic quality of AET's work, including Barbara Perry, who indicated that Mueller "created a large number of relief tiles, some individual, some multi-tile panels. He had a Beaux-Arts style, and his work reveals the influence of the stove tiles he would have been so familiar with in his native Germany. He was partial to classical and Renaissance themes, which worked particularly well with his sculptural style.... Mueller's tenure at AETCo is associated with relief and intaglio tiles and plaques with monochromatic glass glazes that were so popular up to the turn of the century."[14] As mentioned previously, relief tiles included designs that projected out from the base tile, whereas intaglio tiles were indented into the surface of the tile, or, the opposite of the relief tiles.[15] From the technical perspective, Mueller began experimenting with new methods of the application of ceramic tiles to floors and also in creating a more affordable process of creating what he named "mosaic" tiles while he was at AET and from which he wanted to profit in his new business venture.

The two may have previously crossed paths in Cincinnati, as both worked in various potteries over the years, but both ended up at AET, in 1887 (Mueller) and 1890 (Langenbeck). While at AET, both men had attended the 1893 World's Columbian Exposition in Chicago, and they possibly conceived the idea of a new tile company during that trip.[16]

In 1894, just before leaving AET, Langenbeck predicted the future of Zanesville's ceramic industry, and perhaps hinted at his entrepreneurship, while speaking at the Zanesville Board of Trade: "You have raw material inexhaustible. You are known ... to every geologist in the country, who if you will make use of the advertisement, will back up your statements as to your clay, to the capitalists of his acquaintance. And best of all you have a colony of men who have inherited the potter's craft for generations and form the nucleus of an industrial force that you can swell to any number you have a mind to."[17]

What would make their company different? Mueller and Langenbeck brought the scientific and the creative sides of ceramics together and crafted new methods for creating and adhering tiles to any surface. This entrepreneurial "big idea" combined Mueller's invention for manufacturing mosaics, for which he was awarded a patent in 1895, and Langenbeck's new methods of adhering ceramic tiles and building the mechanical tools needed for successful creativity and production.[18]

Mueller's method for creating mosaics, in no small part, was the impetus for the name of the company. Normally, mosaic murals would have been made painstakingly with small, one-sixteenth of an inch, varying colors of tile pieces. Mueller's process created the mosaic effect with multiple colors and shapes directly applied to a larger tile instead of multiple small pieces. The process described simply in the trade publication, *Brick*, was a "method of making an encaustic, or mosaic tile of any desired pattern or combination of colors in a very simple and expeditious way."[19] Mueller's own description of the process was "the art of manufacturing mosaics or of applying colored pigments to the decoration of surfaces."[20] By applying a type of removable metal or cardboard stencil or "cell-plate" to the top of the tile mold, the color of dried powdered clay can be sifted into the specific section of the tile and applied within those cut-out spaces of the stencil.[21] The patterned stencil can be removed, and the next stencil's color applied in its place until the entire piece has been fully covered with the various colors or the final background material. The Kovels, well-known antique authorities, described these as "Florentine mosaic" tiles with a "dull finish … inlaid with colored clays under pressure."[22]

The Mosaic Tile Company's own retrospective documentation indicated that "the tile industry before that time had made inlaid square by the slow and costly method of using separate copper moulds for each color in the design."[23] *Brick* indicated that this method would give "great freedom" to the artist who is no longer "bound by the limits of a pattern book but can order his decorative tiles in exact accordance with his own ideas, both in design and color, without unduly increasing the cost."[24] A single tile could include hundreds or thousands of individual colors instead of multiple small pieces of tile that normally have been used in the creation of mosaic designs, piece by piece. The results of such a design not only saved money but also created "indestructability" by using clay instead of marble when using this method in decorative flooring.[25] Mueller also described this durability in a trade journal in 1903, "Much of the ceramic mosaic is furnished of broken bits of tile, this being the most artistic, as well as most costly, product…. This 'regular' ceramic mosaic offers another decorative possibility…. As this process is accomplished … it is quite cheap and the marble mosaic thus been distanced by its stronger cousin to a remarkable degree."[26]

With these new ideas and a desire for wealth, Langenbeck and Mueller decided to seek financial investors to help realize the dream. On September 4, 1894, the inventors of this new artistic process for ceramic tiles obtained incorporation papers for the newly created Mosaic Tile Company.[27] A few days later, on September 8, 1894, according to a Mosaic Tile Company document, the stockholders met in the city clerk's office in Zanesville.[28] The stockholders elected a Board of Directors including William Bateman, Karl Langenbeck, Perlin Langhan, David Lee, Edmund Moeser, Herman C. Mueller, William Shinnick, C. Stolzenbach, and J. Hope Sutor. (These individuals are the primary stockholders as noted in several resources; however, one source names additional individuals:

J.K. Arnold, Thomas Forgerty, and William E. Miller.[29]) Further, the stakeholders named David Lee as president, William Bateman as vice president, and William Shinnick as secretary and treasurer. Langenbeck and Mueller were also named superintendents. The team also considered a parcel of land for establishing the business; however, it was decided on September 16, 1894, to purchase the property in the southwest corner of the newly plotted Brighton subdivision near the Muskingum County Fairgrounds on Coopermill Road (now Pershing Road).[30]

The Brighton area had been laid out in 1891 by a group of real estate developers and bankers who wanted to profit from the growth of Zanesville.[31] They had purchased a 110-acre farm between the west side of Zanesville (presumably the Putnam area) and the county fairground property. The developers paid for the rail development to be secured in the area, and a streetcar line ran to the county fairgrounds which provided transportation for Mosaic Tile Company employees throughout Zanesville and the county to get to the factory. The company started with only 30 employees in 1894 to 1895 and most needed the streetcar since the automobile had yet to be a major source of transportation in Ohio. Some employees, including Langenbeck and Shinnick, chose to ride horses or use a horse and buggy to get to work.[32]

This land, on which the Mosaic Tile Company's buildings were constructed on a road named Cooper Mill at the time, was described as "low and rather swampy," and would prove to be a challenge in the newly built brick buildings.[33] The initial four buildings included one that "housed the clay preparation room and machine shop. Another … was the boiler house and engine room. The stock shed was the third building, and the fourth contained the press room, kiln shed, and office."[34] It was noted that the swampy land caused the kiln to sink a foot or more into the ground.[35] The company began with only one round kiln with a 10-foot diameter. A *Times Recorder* article reported that employees had memories of water seeping into the kiln and extinguishing the fire.[36] The company then worked to raise the level of the kilns back to the surface of the ground.

Once the buildings were ready Mueller and Langenbeck were eager to put their creative ideas into action, and production officially began in 1895 with 30 employees focusing on six-inch square and hexagon tiles. These floor tiles were made with local buff clay[37] which is a very natural earthy color with content of "materials sufficiently high in iron to fire buff rather than white in color."[38] This tile was in great demand at the time by the building trades due to the rapid growth of commercial and residential buildings in the Midwestern states' expansions. With this utilitarian tile providing a line of profit for the company, Mueller and Langenbeck could experiment with the creative side of the business. It would take time to build the customer base needed to fully support the creative mosaic mural endeavor.

The tile-making process used at the Mosaic Tile Company began catching the attention of the larger industry in trade journals and news articles, which noted their process as different than other companies of the time. For most tiles, the decorative features are applied to the surface of the tile, whereas the encaustic tile created by Mosaic Tile had colors that were more deeply set into body of the tile by using different colors of powdered clays prior to the firing in the kiln. Mueller's mosaic invention required those perforated cards, which were set up like stencils and were created using perforating machines which have been described as similar in size to sewing machines, each operated with a foot pedal. The machines would allow the operators to accurately punch the part of the card with correct spacing to accommodate the different colors. Once the perforated cards were ready, the work began in the "pressing room." This location, in addition to a few other spaces, is often described as one of the locations where the "girls" worked, as noted by the authors who wrote articles and stories in the late 1800s. (Male employees were referred to as operators, and females, as girls or women.) In the pressing room, there was a circular bench which seems reminiscent of an industrial-looking round dining room table. Seated around this rotating bench were the women who were responsible for their portions of the color in the tiles through which their powdered, colorful clays would be inserted. Each tile was placed on the bench, the worker applied her specific colors of clays through the stenciled card, and the table would then rotate to the next person for her colors. When the tile had made it around the entire table, an operator would lift the tile "with a dexterous, straight-up movement, leaving the little mosaics of clay standing undisturbed, side-by-side."[39]

After a clay backing had been applied to the tile, the tile was placed into a hydraulic press, designed by Mueller, and the appropriate pressure was applied with time for allowing air into the tile and the remaining powdered clay to escape.[40] Benefiting from inventions of Langenbeck and Mueller, the company used machines and tools that helped lift the tiles from the press to the sagger which was "a box or case made of refractory baked clay in which the finer ceramic wares are enclosed and protected while baking."[41] The invention that helped lift the tiles has been described as a "pallet of similar construction to a photographic plate holder."[42] This holder allowed the "girl" to carefully pick up the tile and push a "slide" under the tile. The tiles were then "virtually encased in the holder."[43] All of these holders were placed into storage racks at which time the slide was removed. This action was repeated until the sagger was full. The saggers were taken by the operators to the kilns for the appropriate number of days. Langenbeck had designed these kilns, three of which were 20 feet in diameter, with places to stack the wares in the center and doors that were large enough for one man to pass through.[44] After the time expired, the saggers were removed from the kilns and taken to the sorting room "where many girls are employed in sorting the small pieces as to color and quality."[45]

Without the convenience of today's instant communication, Mueller and Langenbeck needed to rely on advertisements in local papers, trade journals, and their own sales trips to spread the word of their creations. As superintendents of the company, at least one of them needed to stay at the factory to maintain the daily work. In addition to serving as the designer and chemist, the two also had to "invent and design machinery, and they purchased materials and employed workmen."[46] Langenbeck and Mueller also took turns traveling the country to bolster sales. These trips focused on potential customers and with architectural contacts that they had developed. The competition for these accounts in the tile business was fierce, and they needed to personally show and describe their products and methods. Their travels also helped keep them current with the newest trends in the building industry and customer demand.

Mueller and Langenbeck created a method of applying their tiles to withstand high traffic on floors and to provide permanency on walls and ceilings; the process was patented in 1900. Sometimes referred to as "Plicaro cement," the invention was described in the patent application as a "tile floor, wall, or ceiling which will not crack either from the settling of the building or from the jarring and which may be applied upon ordinary floors or walls without the application of heavy substructures … accomplished by forming the backing of flexible tough materials, which while it holds the tile tenaciously in place, yet adjusts itself to a change of the position of the floor."[47] This process could be used directly on an existing floor, so no additional construction need occur. The key to the patent was the mixture of the cement's composition: "Made up of pieces of a material of a hard resisting nature bound together at the joints by a material similar to that of a backing ... hard resisting material set into a backing which rises into the joints between the pieces and sets from a plastic to a flexible tough state."[48] Able to withstand time, heavy foot traffic, and wear and tear of a building, the Plicaro method gave Mueller and Langenbeck the canvas they needed to create beautiful designs and murals using their tilework.

Back at the factory, in 1898, as production increased, abundant supplies of clay were needed.[49] From the local area, buff clay from Ellis Station just a few miles away from the factory had been used along with other clay delivered via the Belt Line Railway Company to the Brighton area. Ellis Station was part of the Cincinnati & Muskingum Valley Railway in 1870 in the northern part of Muskingum County. Shortly after that line was built, one of the canal locks of the Muskingum River was located at Ellis Station. It was also the site of a post office for the area.[50] Having started with one kiln, the company added three round kilns to accommodate varying sizes of tiles. Adapting to the needs of the building trades, Mosaic Tile added plain wall and trim tile for wainscoting. While still attempting to focus on creative ventures, the company needed to add more practical options as demands changed over time.

Around 1898, the company decided that the growth of the plain utilitarian tiles and tiles that were of a dull finish which were "inlaid with colored clays" created with pressure, as they did with the mosaic decorative tiles, necessitated a branch office in New York City.[51] In 1902, the company also leased a plant at Matawan Tile Company in New Jersey to accommodate the growing demand for production in the eastern part of the U.S.[52]

Langenbeck and Mueller left the Mosaic Tile Company, which they had begun just nine years prior, in 1903, perhaps in a disagreement with other company leaders or disenchanted by the fading dream of mosaic mural tile works. The artistic interest and demand for decorative mural tile work had slowed and the sales of the company shifted to account for the demand for 6-inch square and 6-inch hexagonal floor tile.[53] Mueller first moved to Pennsylvania to the Robertson Art Tile Company and, in 1908, he opened his own Mueller Mosaic Company in New Jersey.[54] Langenbeck accepted a job at the Tariff Commission and National Bureau of Standards in Washington, D.C.[55]

Without the visionary leaders at the helm, the company turned to William Shinnick, Jr., to take on greater responsibility. Originally serving as secretary and treasurer, Shinnick became the general manager around 1907.[56] Shinnick had been born in Zanesville in 1846 and grew up with his father working in the contracting and manufacturing business.[57] The younger Shinnick joined him initially in that business and the duo worked on "material improvement of the city" in the early days.[58] Shinnick's civic mindedness led him to positions at the City of Zanesville: Secretary of the city water works, city clerk, and assistant postmaster.[59] In 1878, he was elected as member of the City School Board of Education. He held that position for 27 years and served in leadership positions of president, treasurer, and clerk of the board. He also served as the first secretary of the county workhouse board and secretary of the cemetery board for 10 years.

Moving on from the Mueller and Langenbeck era, and into the Shinnick-led period, growth within the facilities of the Mosaic Tile Company's Zanesville location occurred. A historical sketch of the Mosaic Tile Company in a 1943 newspaper article indicated that

Watercolor painting of Mosaic Tile Company plant, 1905, by Andrew Loomis (courtesy Ohio History Connection (OVS710.tif))

during this time, in the early 1900s, the company also leased a small pottery plant, the Muskingum Stoneware Company, in the Putnam area.[60] This location focused on the colorful glazed tile for which the company had the most demand at the time. The lease, however, expired in 1903, and the company moved the work back to the Pershing Road plant. To accommodate this work, in 1904, the company added a second floor to one of the original four buildings and, in 1905, added four new buildings.[61] In addition to the increased production, the new space was needed to accommodate heavy machinery on the plant floor. The Company acquired an additional three acres of land when the original five-acre site ran out of room. "Three or four" buildings were constructed for the specific use of manufacturing glazed tiles and new office locations were removed from the older buildings into the newer.[62] Starting in 1906, Mosaic began manufacturing glazed wall tile.[63]

Shinnick is credited with leading the company in its largest growth starting in 1907.[64] He took on the role of general manager and changed processes that had been Mueller's preferred methods. One example was when Shinnick began using the dry press process which continued to be in use until at least the mid–1940s. In this process, the clay materials were "blended and mixed in water by blunger mills."[65] A blunger mill is a machine for mixing clay by hand or with electricity.[66] By the late 1920s, the company indicated that production distribution was 50 percent on wall tile and trim, 35 percent on ceramic mosaic floor tile, and 10 to 15 percent on vitreous tile.[67] During the next decade, Shinnick added 16 new hand presses, which were eventually converted to automatic tile presses run by electricity.[68]

The Company, along with the rest of Ohio, faced a significant challenge in March of 1913. A great flood, brought on by three days of heavy rainfall, caused the major rivers in the state to overflow, with the Muskingum River rising 27 feet above the flood stage.[69] Over 400 people died in Ohio and damage to homes and businesses was

Mosaic Tile Company postcard, 1909.

widespread.[70] While the flood damage was concentrated along the rivers and especially damaging to structures in the downtown Zanesville and Putnam areas, with 20-foot-deep waters at street intersections, the outlying Brighton district was also affected.[71] The flood's ripple effect forced the company to shut down operations due to the stoppage of clean water and gas supplies and train service from March through the beginning of May.[72]

Surviving that natural catastrophe, business was going well for the Mosaic Tile Company as it continued to produce the wall and floor tiles in demand in the building industry. The Company had installed their first two tunnel kilns in 1917 and was beginning to experiment with faience tile manufacturing.[73] Faience is described as a "fine glazed earthenware, usually with a colorful decoration."[74] In comparison to round "beehive" kilns, tunnel kilns provided an efficiency improvement of decreased time to fire the ware from 7 days to 48 hours.[75] As for faience tile, sources have cited a variety of original locations where this technique began. One source indicated that the town of Faenza, Italy "was one of the early centers of the manufacture of faience."[76] The Kovels indicated that Mosaic Tile Company produced faience wall tiles in a variety of pastel colors.[77]

Just as these new enhancements came about, the United States was faced with major disruptions. First, the country entered World War I in mid–1917. With about 20 employees leaving Mosaic to serve in the military and due to a great slow-down of the building industry, the company operated on a restricted basis until the end of the war on November 11, 1918.[78] Just as the world was moving toward peace, the next disruption was the outbreak of the Spanish flu of 1918. Although no one knows for certain, this pandemic was thought to have been brought from Europe to the United States by returning soldiers. This deadly disease affected millions worldwide. No known resources specifically mention how the Spanish flu impacted Mosaic Tile, but newspaper accounts from Zanesville in 1918 through 1920 showed a progressive wave of illnesses and deaths in the area.[79]

The company's first quarter of a century of incorporation started with the entrepreneurial spirit of Langenbeck and Mueller and ended with the business- and civic-minded leadership of Shinnick. The final historical events of these early years led into the next era of the company during which Mosaic Tile Company became one of the largest tile producers in the world.

Significant Works During this Time Period

During those first few years of incorporation, the Mosaic Tile Company completed several large projects using Mueller's decorative mosaic method as well some more utilitarian floor covering. These are mentioned here to capture the historical time period of the Company and will be described in more detail in their respective chapters based on locations which illustrate the far geographical reach of this company based in Zanesville.

One of the first large scale murals to be showcased was designed and created by Mueller in 1898. The Zanesville's St. Nicholas Catholic Church featured a Christopher Columbus scene landing in the new world along with angels overlooking the entryway and a date referencing the completion of the work. The Mosaic Tile Company is also credited in books and articles in these early years with involvement in the construction of the new Library of Congress in Washington, D.C. (1897); the Grant and Garfield school buildings in Zanesville (1896); the Cincinnati Market House (1898); the Fort Wayne (Allen County), Indiana Courthouse (1897–1902); the Hotel Rogge in Zanesville (1900); the Holland Tunnel in New York City (1901); the California State Capitol (1906); and the Panama Canal (1904–1914) among others.

4

World War I through 1928

Recovering from the destructive flood of 1913, the next couple of decades for the Mosaic Tile Company were a time of rebound and growth. During and after these major events, the company added kilns and began new types of tile manufacturing. Shipments to countries around the world flourished at a fast pace, a branch office was opened, and competing tile companies were purchased to meet the heightened demand for tile products. This growth, primarily overseen by leader William Shinnick, gave the company a great advantage over other companies, as they were building the company's reputation and reach.

Just prior to World War I, as mentioned previously, the company began manufacturing faience tile with the addition of tunnel kilns. Tunnel kilns, in comparison to the traditional "beehive" kilns, are nonstationary, because the tile products are inserted at one end on a wheeled sagger or other cart and then pushed or pulled along through the tunnel to the other end at the appropriate speed and heat needed for the product.[1] In the early versions of tunnel kilns the heat sources, combustion fuels such as coal, remain stationary, while the product travels through preheating, firing, and cooling stages. Oil and gas burners had been introduced into the tunnel kilns between 1900 and 1920, and this proved to be more economical and produced more uniform tiles "because they were less reliant on human tending of the fuel."[2] Mosaic's two tunnel kilns were 300 feet and 225 feet in length. The longer kiln was for bisque tile (or biscuit, at it is usually called) and the other was for gloss tile.[3] Bisque tile is made of a "clay that has been hardened through a first firing. Bisque ware can be left undecorated."[4] Each kiln "is claimed to be the equal of 10 periodical [beehive] kilns, thus giving the plant the equivalent of 50 beehive type kilns."[5] Further, the efficiency improves productivity as "each kiln will turn out a truck of ware every hour or hour and a half."[6]

With such kilns in place, Mosaic produced enough tile to keep up with demand for the floor and wall tiles, in addition to their new line of satin wall matte tile at that time. For clarity, a satin finish on tile is defined as having a slight sheen which, when viewed a certain angle, will offer a small amount of light reflection.[7] A matt or matte finish is described as a flat glaze finish without gloss.[8] The local newspaper reported that Mosaic was "one of very few companies that turns out a full line of floor, wall, decorative, and artistic or faience tile."[9] Mosaic was not only supplying companies within the United States, Canada, and Mexico, but they were shipping products to South America, Japan, Australia, China, Russia, Central America, and Cuba.[10] By the late 1910s, the company had opened branch offices in New York, Chicago, San Francisco, and St. Louis in order to have employees serving those large metropolitan areas.[11]

In the 1920s, the company branched out to add accessories to go with floor and wall tiles for the bathroom and kitchen. This included a line of bathroom accessories such as toothbrush holder, towel racks, hooks, soap dishes, and more to complement the other tiles in the room. Up to this time, all bathroom and residential tile in the industry was white.[12]

At this point in the company's history, Mosaic Tile was one of the largest producers of ceramic tiles in the country. The company added another nine kilns to address the demand for the utilitarian tiles in Zanesville while it acquired the Atlantic Tile Manufacturing Company in New Jersey to help with production on the east coast in 1920.[13] Atlantic Tile had "a distinctive glazing style that you can recognize by the satin or matte finish as well as more artisanal finish that isn't totally opaque like other tile companies."[14] An artisanal finish is described as a high-quality or distinctive product made in small quantities, usually by hand or using traditional methods.[15] At the time of purchase, Atlantic Tile had one round kiln and was only making floor tile. Mosaic dramatically increased their production by adding 10 round kilns. Eventually, Mosaic removed the round kilns and instead added tunnel kilns.

In 1922, matte and bright glazed tile were introduced by Mosaic Tile in pastel colors, which was about three years before other companies offered competition.[16] The pastel and bright glaze tiles were in great demand, and it was estimated that just one of the tunnel kilns produced 20,000 feet of tile in a week's time, but it was still not enough to meet the demand.[17]

In the midst of this growth at Mosaic Tile, William Shinnick died in 1923. Shinnick had always been a civic-minded individual and had served in multiple roles with the city of Zanesville and the city school's board of education. Several organizations in the Zanesville area still benefit from the bequests that Shinnick generously identified in his estate. Just before Shinnick's death, he and his wife, Dr. Anna Hill Shinnick, "founded the Shinnick Trust Fund through the assignment of their property to the First Trust and Savings Bank."[18] When he died a couple of months later, his wife "ordered that distribution of the income should start at once, rather than after her own death, to the Zanesville Welfare Association, Day Nursery, Helen Purcell Home, Bethesda Hospital, and Shinnick Educational Fund."[19] A newspaper article later reported (in 1973) that the trust funds equaled between $2 and $3 million, much of which was made up of Mosaic Tile Company stocks.[20] His obituary proudly declared that Shinnick's "clear vision saw the future of Zanesville and with faith in that future he directed his efforts along lines which won for him material prosperity and contributed in no small degree to the welfare of the community."[21]

After the death of the company's leader, the remaining management continued to expand. By 1925, the company had 1,250 employees, added more tunnel kilns, bought more land, and built more facilities.[22] At this point, the company was capable of producing any kind of tile and indeed produced the largest of its volume in the company history in the years of 1925 to 1927.[23] After having had a strong presence in New York City for several years, a dedicated building was constructed in 1928 for the company's offices.[24] This building, at 445 West 41st Street, was seven stories tall and featured a grand amount of mural tile work on the façade. The company name was installed using tiles across the top of the three large first floor windows. Above each of the next six floors' windows, the design included tiles in circle- and diamond-shaped designs. At the roof, tiles covered the front of the roofline with half circles and plain tiles. Only a black and white photo survives of the building in the Kovels' 1974 and 1993 books.[25] Unfortunately, this building was demolished in 1954 and now apartment buildings are in its place.

William Shinnick gravesite, Woodlawn Cemetery.

Mosaic Tile Company was taking its place as the leader in the nation in the Roaring Twenties, all while building its foundation in the small town of Zanesville, Ohio. Unfortunately, the nation was about to experience an economic crisis that no company or person could have imagined.

Significant Works During this Time Period

In the late 1910s and early 1920s, the first large order of color wall tile was for the Henry Ford Hospital in Detroit. The order included "85,000 square feet of wall tile and 60,000 pieces of trim tile."[26] Furthermore, the company continued to fulfill large orders within significant architectural structures such as the Stevens Hotel in Chicago, at the time the world's largest hotel, built in 1925.

Scorpio Zodiac tile.

Water Crane "Aesop's Fables" tiles.

Omar Khayyam *Rubaiyat* tiles.

Green pitcher (courtesy Muskingum County History).

Swan White coasters (courtesy Jeffrey Snyder).

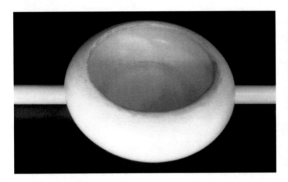

Yellow bowl.

Pink bowl.

Floral coasters (multicolor).

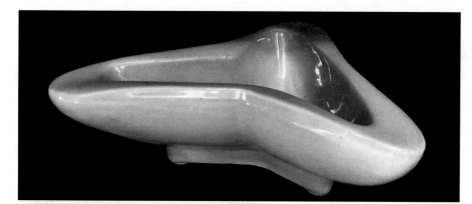

Green ashtray.

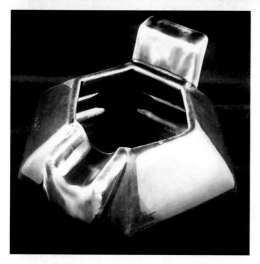

Racetrack oval ashtray (courtesy Muskingum County History).

Smokestack ashtray.

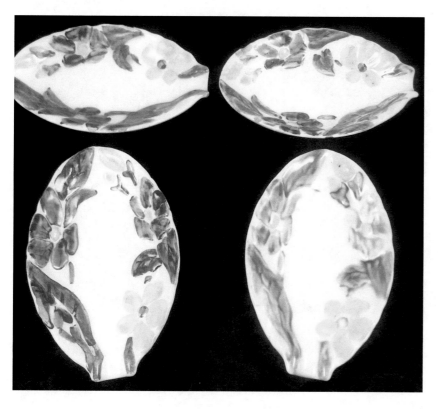

Floral ashtrays.

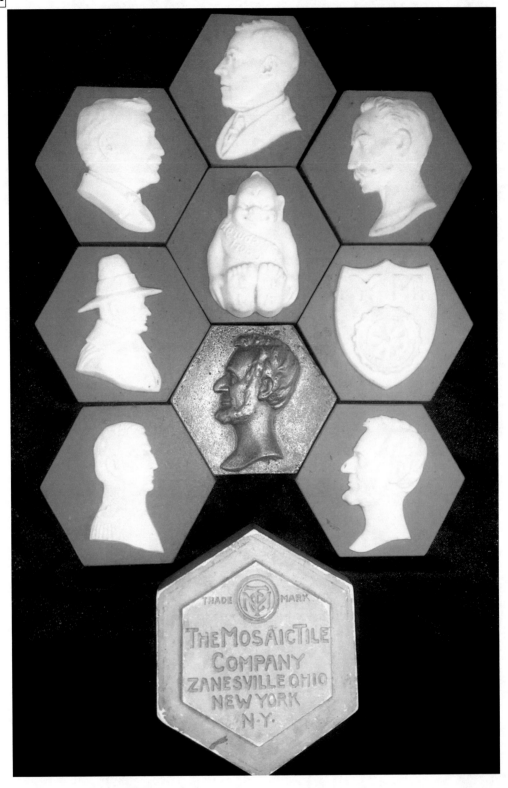

Hexagonal Jasperware paperweights: (from bottom left) Simon Bolivar, Robert Treat, David Lloyd George, Woodrow Wilson, Jose Marti, New York Rotary, Abraham Lincoln, Abraham Lincoln (cast iron), Billiken. Bottom: plastic mold—reverse image of typical mark on hexagonal paperweights.

Benjamin Franklin hexagonal paperweight (courtesy David M. Taylor).

OERBA hexagonal paperweight (courtesy David M. Taylor).

General John Pershing oval paperweight.

George Washington oval paperweight (courtesy David M. Taylor).

Round paperweights: Zanesville Sesquicentennial, the Mosaic Tile Company's W.V. Stafford, Bethesda Hospital (in blue and yellow), Good Samaritan Hospital, various Mosaic Tile products, Rotary International, and William M. Shinnick.

Terrier tray.

Bear figure.

Lying and sitting German shepherds.

Pink turtle trinket box.

Child fountain (courtesy Muskingum County History).

Green globe.

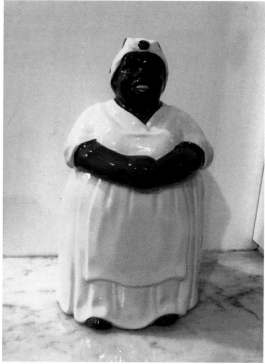

Cookie jar (courtesy Joey Osborn).

Station of the Cross V (courtesy Jeff Koehler, Koehler Auctions).

Station of the Cross XII (courtesy Pastor Tara Mitchell, Central Presbyterian Church).

Bird images.

5

The Great Depression through 1960

As the United States ended the Roaring Twenties and approached the 1930s, the Great Depression brought the mood of the nation from frivolity to despair with many suffering from unemployment, poverty, rationing, and depression. By 1933, 15 million Americans were unemployed, and nearly half of the U.S. banks had failed.[1] Inaugurated in 1933, President Franklin Delano Roosevelt worked with Congress to pass reform legislation to reopen banks, "to stabilize industrial and agricultural production, create jobs, and stimulate recovery."[2] By the end of the '30s, there was hope for the nation's recovery. At the time, the average cost of living was $4,000 per year, the annual average salary was $1,125, and the average house cost $5,472.[3]

Mosaic Tile Company had employed over 1,200 employees in 1925, and it is unclear how many were still employed in the early 1930s.[4] As the Great Depression engulfed businesses and individuals, the company operated on a limited basis and had employees working on facility improvement as company leaders anticipated future economic recovery and tile orders to resume. The company had suffered losses as the building industry greatly declined, as many were out of work and could not afford to build, and companies could not invest in infrastructure.[5] The Zanesville plant decreased work to three days per week and even on those days, some of the time was spent on making improvements to the facilities rather than producing tiles for customers who at the time did not exist. During this slow down, the company also began to manufacture hot plates or trivets, "wall panels, souvenirs, and brooches [sic]."[6] The employees making these items experimented with new decoration such as silk screening, hand painting, outlining in black between glazes of different colors, and adding "sunk and raised patterns, underglaze and overglaze."[7] Underglaze is applied on unglazed ware and then glaze is applied over the paint.[8] Overglaze is applied on the ware then paint is applied on top of the glaze.[9]

The company attempted to keep as many employees as possible during this trying time with hopes of returning to the regular production of tiles as soon as the Great Depression was over. The leaders of Mosaic Tile were right in their vision that the company would rebound. By the mid–1930s, the company had acquired additional plants and was involved in major tile installations across the nation. It could be that the Great Depression was too much for the other companies to withstand, and Mosaic Tile Company was financially able to make the most of the situation. These plants continued to help widen Mosaic Tile's reach throughout the country. In 1935, Mosaic bought the Carlyle Tile Company of Ironton, Ohio, which had operated as a quarry, tile and brick plant and, from that point forward, the Carlyle plant strictly manufactured tile.[10] Two years later, in 1937, Mosaic purchased controlling interest in the General Tile Corporation in El Segundo, California.[11]

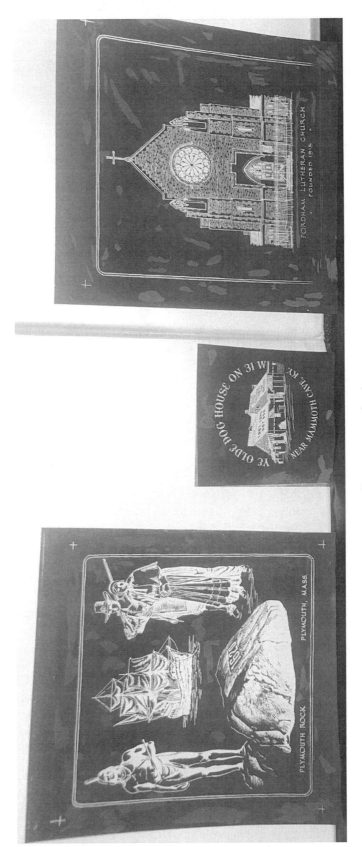

Silk screen transfer sheets.

A 1939 sales catalog provided an in-depth look at the products Mosaic Tile was manufacturing as well as boasting of several large projects using their products.[12] A few lavish residential homes in Florida and Chicago were mentioned along with schools, churches, and hospitals. The company also promoted their work with large swimming pools in Ohio and Michigan and laboratories at Mellon Institute in Pittsburgh. Exterior store fronts are featured with "faience tile in large units" which claimed to be weatherproof and easy to maintain.[13] Along with these products, the company showed diversification with fireplace mantels, fountains, and additional bathroom accessories.

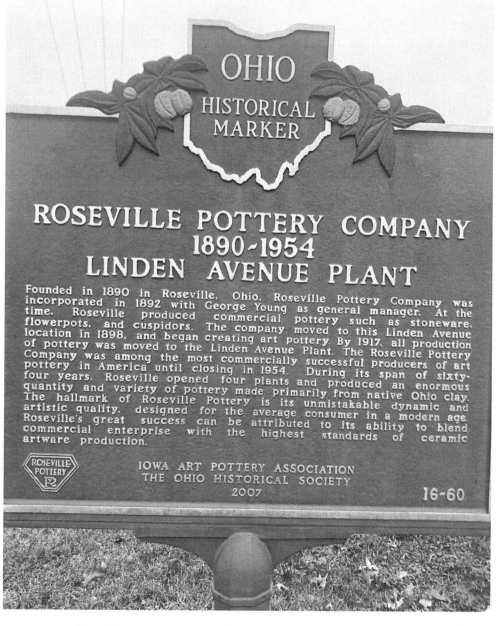

Roseville Pottery Company, historical marker on Linden Avenue.

In their 1944 "Fiftieth Anniversary Program," Mosaic Tile Company claimed that it ranked "as the largest tile factory in the United States."[14] At that time, the buildings and property covered thirty acres of ground in the Brighton subdivision, while the floor space within the manufacturing buildings was about six acres.[15] During the late 1930s and early 1940s, the company experienced its largest growth when the number of employees rose to more than 1,400 by 1947.[16]

The '50s era brought expansion and innovation for the Mosaic Tile Company. In 1954, the competing Roseville Pottery Company closed its production and its building on Linden Avenue in Zanesville was sold to the Mosaic Tile Company.[17] Roseville Pottery originally began in Roseville in 1892 and had focused on jars, flowerpots, and spittoons (or cuspidors).[18] The company had moved to Zanesville and had created multiple art pottery lines that are highly prized by collectors today.

The company continued to be innovative as evidenced in a 1952 patent application for "Electrically-Conductive Ceramic Floor-Tile Units and Floors Composed of Such Conductive Units."[19] Created by George Ford and Otto Kauffman, a German chemical engineer, the description indicated that this type of floor-tile unit and floor reduced static electricity by minimizing electrical conductivity.[20] (Author's note: As mentioned in the Preface, Mr. Kauffmann and his family lived in a home in southern Muskingum County which the family decorated with hundreds of Mosaic Tile product in the 1950s. This home has been the family home of the author and is currently under restoration.) The ability to avoid static electricity was incredibly important for hospital operating rooms, nuclear and electrical laboratories, and other manufacturing laboratories where the danger of igniting combustible materials existed and could cause accidents and deaths. The patent for the product was approved in 1958, just two years after the company had utilized

Good Samaritan Hospital postcard, circa 1950s.

it in a new seven-story addition at Zanesville's Good Samaritan Hospital in 1956. Used throughout the hospital, on floors and walls in the kitchen, "scrub-up" areas, and operating rooms, Mosaic advertised it as "Imperviously Electrically Conductive Ceramic Mosaic Tile, which reduces the danger of anesthesia explosion due to electrostatic spark or electrical shock."[21]

The company finished out the 1950s with a new focus on do-it-yourself home decorators. According to a 1957 newspaper article, 64 percent of homes built in the United States used ceramic tile.[22] The company was counting on the '60s to bring additional opportunities for growth. Planning for that, perhaps, the company applied for another patent in 1959 for a method of joining small tiles together with paper-backing that was

Mosaic Tile Company, sheet of tiles.

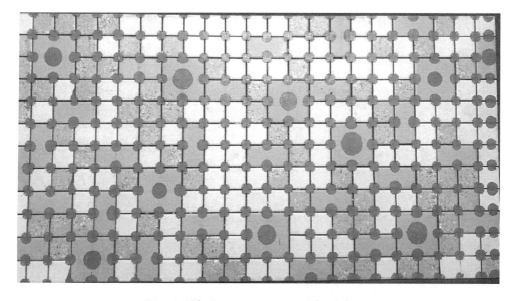

Mosaic Tile Company, reverse side of sheet.

easy to use and intended to be flexible enough to not need uniform evenness on the
base floor. Called "Multiple Unit Ceramic Tile Assembly," this makes tile work easier for
"do-it-yourself ceramic tile floors" that previously would not have been feasible.[23] This
type of paper-backing had been available for some time; however, Mosaic's proposed
backing was a "resinous mass" that tightly adhered to the back of the tile surface and
remained flexible.[24] The resin covered only a small space on the back of the tile to allow
for maximum exposure to the bonding materials. This forward-thinking invention prepared the company to appeal to the previously untapped market of do-it-yourself homeowners who wanted to add to their current homes or to save money during construction.
This foresight seemed to bode well for the company in leading them into the 1960s.

Significant Works During this Time Period

In 1936, the Mosaic Tile Company was employed to create a large-scale mural display in Fort Worth, Texas, for the newly built Will Rogers Coliseum and Auditorium,
in commemoration of the Texas centennial. Additional large-scale projects during these
decades included the luxury liner, S.S. *America* (1939); the White House Library fireplace
mantel (1945); and the Pace-Setter home in New York (1951).

In the Zanesville area, projects included the mural and flooring of the brand new
Municipal Auditorium in Zanesville (1940); the renovated exterior of the Williams Bakery on Market Street (1947); the altar in the Baker Chapel within the St. John's Lutheran
Church on Seventh Street (1950); the newly designed exterior of the Ohio Fuel Gas Company's building on Fourth Street (1951); the remodeling at the YMCA for the "Teen Tyme"
room (1951); the modern J.C. Penney retail store in the downtown area (1953); a new
Zanesville High School on Blue Avenue (1954); the exterior mural on a new section of
the *Times Recorder* building (1958); and the new building for the congregation of the First
Evangelical United Brethren church (1959).

6

1960 through the Closing
of the Zanesville Facility

The company started strong in the 1960s with the continued surge in home building. In Memphis, Tennessee, Mosaic opened a new showroom which brought the total to 40 customer-focused centers throughout the United States.[1] These centers featured a broad line of glazed wall tile, ceramic mosaic patterns, quarry tile, and tile setters' tools and materials for the do-it-yourselfers.

One such creation intended for ambitious homeowners by the company was described earlier in a patent application filed in 1959 and approved in 1962. The first application, for the "Multiple Unit Ceramic Tile Assembly" was created by Herbert Macdonald, David Barbour and Karl M. Claus.[2] The follow-up patent application, submitted in 1961 and approved in 1965, was for the "Method of Fabricating a Multiple Unit Assembly" and was created by Macdonald, Barbour, and Claus along with Robert Cleverly.[3] This application was a "carrying forward of the invention of the previous application ... not only for the production of such modular multiple unit tile assemblies, but also the production of multiple unit assemblies of larger size."[4] The intention was to allow the versatility of laying sheets of tiles by homeowners who were not as familiar with the complexities of laying and cementing other types of sheets of tiles.

All small towns have local gossip and with a business that employed so many of its residents, the local newspaper shared information about an illness that suddenly overwhelmed seven women in the pasting department at the factory in April 1962. The paper indicated that the women were overcome with headaches, nausea, numbness, and chills and were taken to Bethesda Hospital for treatment. The newspaper, obviously operating under pre–Health Insurance Portability and Accountability Act of 1996 (HIPAA) rules, reported details about the women, including their names, ages, and home addresses.[5] In an effort to figure out what made the women ill, the company brought in canaries to "determine the potency of fumes that might exist in mines and the like."[6] Dating back to 1911 in Britain, canaries would be taken into mines with the coal miners to test for carbon monoxide gas.[7] If the canaries died, that gave the miners enough time to evacuate the mine. This practice was common in Great Britain, Canada, and the United States until the mid–1980s when an electrical technique would be substituted.[8] For this mystery at the Mosaic Tile Company, the canaries "showed no ill effects," and the women were dismissed from the hospital without knowing exactly what caused their illness.[9]

In 1962, a key move occurred that may have foretold the future. The company moved the executive offices from Zanesville to Cleveland in August of that year. In a newspaper article that was focused on the promotions of two employees, a short message was buried within the article referring to these employees being connected to the move of the head-quarters "to Cleveland when Mosaic's executive offices are relocated there."[10] No other information can be found about any announcements of this move or anything that may have precipitated it. This move may have been a hint at a decrease in the reliance on the Zanesville facility.

Within just a year of this move, the United States Tariff Commission released a report about ceramic imports in November 1963. This report followed an extensive investigation into requests by ceramic workers for adjustment assistance under the Trade Expansion Act of 1962 alleging that "increasing imports of ceramic mosaic tile caused in major part by concessions granted under trade agreements were the major factor causing unemployment or underemployment to a significant number of employees" of the Winburn Tile Manufacturing Company of Little Rock Arkansas, a subsidiary of the Mosaic Tile Company of Cleveland, Ohio.[11]

This was an important factor in the future of the company and the ceramic industry. Imports into the U.S. of ceramic products were increasing and possibly causing unemployment; however, the Tariff Commission disagreed with the claim and found that tile was not being imported to the point of hurting businesses. In fact, the commission found that Winburn had greater than average production and that sales were about the same in 1963 as they had been in 1961 just after a strike in Zanesville had occurred and the Winburn plant picked up the slack in operations. The commission did not, however, disagree that imports were potentially causing competition. Instead, the report indicated that it did not find a "significant number or proportion of the workers are unemployed or underemployed primarily because of increased imports of an article like or direct competition with that produced by Winburn."[12]

By 1966, the company released the announcement from the Cleveland office that the Zanesville plant would close within the year for "economic reasons."[13] At that point, 600 employees were working at the Pershing Road plant. Amazingly, even in the same article with the closing of the Zanesville plant, the newspaper still touted Mosaic Tile as the "largest producer of ceramic tile" in this time period.[14] Apparently that recognition did not spare the Zanesville plant from closing after 70 years in existence.

In March 1967, the Marmon Group acquired the interests and assets of the Mosaic Tile Company. Marmon was owned by the Pritzker family of Chicago with interests in hotels, metal and plastic displays, castings, office partitions, mining equipment, gears, and others.[15] By this time the Zanesville plant had slowed operations and downsized to 150 employees.[16] The Marmon Group reported that the Zanesville plant had experienced losses of over $2 million in 1966 before and after the announcement of the closing.[17] By June of 1967, all Mosaic's Zanesville properties had been sold to Ray Park of Portland, Oregon.[18] He reported to the local newspaper that he wanted to attract new ceramic businesses into the area to use the facilities.[19] Park also confirmed that he would take possession of the buildings by July 30 and all work for Mosaic Tile Company would end on the same date.[20]

In 1968, Marmon had sold the assets of Mosaic Tile Company, including all the plants and sales centers nationwide, to the Stylon Corporation of Milford, Massachusetts, which was a producer of ceramic wall tile and bathroom accessories.[21] Meanwhile, Ray Park had managed to lease space in the Pershing Road buildings to McGraw-Edison Power Systems Division, Dura Corporation, and Stewart-Glapat Corporation, along with 150,000 square feet remaining leased to Marmon.[22] Park was working to make improvements by extensively remodeling and painting the buildings.[23] A new era was beginning for the property on Pershing Road after 73 years as the Mosaic Tile Company.

Significant Works During this Time Period

Even as the company seemed to be winding down, progress was continued, and major projects were taken on. For example, in the local area, the Dillon Dam was a major feature and Mosaic Tile Company was involved in that project (1960). Further, a local business, the Morris and Snyder Tire Company (1962), was supplied with creative automobile images. Further away, in Florida, there was a unique architectural construction of a round building, the KenAnn Building, which reflected images of the surrounding beauty of the ocean (1964).

7

The Sad State of the Company's
Property in the 21st Century

With the company stock acquired by the Marmon Group and the land purchased by Ray Park, the Mosaic Tile Company in Zanesville came to an end. Just as Mosaic Tile had acquired other companies over the years, now was the Marmon Group's turn to buy and sell the Mosaic Tile Company stock. Marmon, which owned a diverse line of properties and products, sold the assets of Mosaic Tile Company to the Stylon Corporation of Boston in 1968. Stylon was cited by the *Times Recorder* as a "producer of ceramic wall tile and bathroom accessories."[1]

Stylon Corporation continued to use the Mosaic Tile Company name as one of their divisions and employed the existing Mosaic Tile executive staff in Cleveland. An additional 1,000 employees were maintained at the other seven manufacturing locations that MTC had previously acquired.[2] Stylon's work with Mosaic Tile seems to have ceased when a merger occurred between Stylon Corporation and DCA Development Corporation in 1969. DCA was known as a "fast moving glamour company … and recipient of hundreds of millions of dollars in urban renewal funds" and was in the business of building federally supported low-income housing.[3] This merger "backfired and served only to further weaken DCA's dwindling resources."[4] DCA filed for bankruptcy in 1973, and there ended the original Mosaic Tile Company.

The Mosaic Tile property on Pershing Road has outlasted the name of the company and has had many owners in the more than 50 years since Mosaic closed. A review of the ownership changes and the deeds, surveys, mortgages, and other legal documentation on the Muskingum County Auditor and Recorder offices' electronic files was quite complex. What appeared to be an owner with one name changed just a short time later to another owner with perhaps a similar name or a company that the other person had acquired. Additionally, the land that Mosaic Tile Company owned totaled more than 15 parcels.[5] Some transactions included all parcels while others were handled separately. The following information attempts to properly attribute ownership of the property over the years with some liberty taken in order to be as concise as possible.

Park, the new owner of the property, started a business partnership with William Graham and, in 1971, Graham purchased Park's part of the ownership.[6] Later that year, Graham reported additional tenants leasing space in the Pershing Road property mostly for storage and warehousing: General Electric, Buckeye Carpet, Mumper Partition, Port-O-Let, Stewart-Glapat Corporation, and Dura Corporation.[7] Also, Continental Rubber Works leased 18,000 square feet for 50 employees manufacturing vacuum hose assemblies for the auto industry.[8]

After the late 1960s, very little information was found regarding the other plants and showrooms that Mosaic had owned around the country. Articles in the local paper would bring up Mosaic Tile in various retrospective pieces, especially around the anniversary dates of the company or of the Zanesville community.[9] Otherwise, there were the occasional notices of companies leasing space within the old buildings.

In 1977, Graham and, what appears to be his business, Graham Investment Group, partnered with Buckeye Carpet Mills, Inc., to sell the property.[10] Buckeye Carpet Mills had leased space in the buildings from Graham starting in 1969. Records are incomplete when Buckeye and Graham formed a partnership related to the property. Nevertheless, the partners sold the property to Mosaic Industrial Properties in 1977.[11] Interestingly, a few of the people who signed the mortgage and deed documents were the same for both Buckeye and Mosaic Industrial Properties.

Less than 10 years later, Mosaic Industrial Properties sold the property to the Akro Corporation.[12] Akro, a floor mat manufacturer for homes and cars, owned the property through 2001 when, at that point, the company had changed its name to Collins & Aikman Accessory Mats, Inc.[13] Only two years later, in 2003, Collins & Aikman sold to Catfish, LLC.[14] Catfish, LLC had multiple addresses noted on county office documents including in Maryland, North Carolina, and Virginia. Catfish, LLC was also connected to the Pelican Land Holdings, LLC, which owned another property in Zanesville, on Linden Avenue, that was part of the old American Encaustic Tiling Company.[15] Catfish, LLC did not respond to efforts to seek information about the future plans for the property.

Catfish, LLC hired a company to demolish the Pershing Road buildings, about the same time that their partner company, Pelican Land Holdings, LLC, hired a demolition company to raze the old American Encaustic Tiling Company site on Linden Avenue in 2015.[16] According to City of Zanesville's former Director of Community Development, Jay Bennett, the demolition was halted when the company failed to obtain the proper permits from the city for the demolition.[17] Not only does this property lay within the City of Zanesville but also within the Brighton Historic District, and various requirements of both were not met. This abrupt cessation of work left the property with partially razed and stripped brick buildings, acres of piled bricks, concrete and debris, all with potentially hazardous materials exposed. A chain-link fence with "no trespassing" signs is barely standing around the perimeter with multiple gaps. Stories of local children exploring and homeless adults seeking refuge in the extremely dangerous buildings occasionally have been reported.[18]

Catfish, LLC, stopped paying the property taxes for the old Mosaic Tile property after early 2014.[19] By late 2020, according to a search on the Muskingum County Auditor's Office website, Catfish, LLC had become delinquent on tax payments amounting to over $82,000 for the largest parcel (approximately 15.5 acres) and hundreds of dollars for each of the several smaller parcels.[20] Additionally, records showed that Catfish, LLC had worked with three banks since 2003 for mortgages on the property: In 2003 through 2005, North Valley Bank; 2005 through 2008, Zions First National Bank; and 2007 through the end of the records in 2017, Century National Bank.[21] Each mortgage released Catfish, LLC from the previous mortgage and began a new debt. In 2019, Century National Bank, in conjunction with the Muskingum County Sheriff's office, placed the property for Sheriff's Sale of Real Estate which had been scheduled for February 14, 2019.[22] According to communication from the Sheriff's office, there were no bids on the

Mosaic Tile Company property, 2020, westside facing Dryden Road.

Mosaic Tile Company property, 2020, eastside facing Lexington Avenue.

Mosaic Tile Company property, 2020, northside facing Dryden Road.

Mosaic Tile Company property, 2020, southside facing Pershing Road.

property, so it did not sell.[23] The Muskingum County Sheriff's office suggested reaching out to the mortgage holding bank, previously known as Century National Bank, which responded that the bank was unable to provide information.[24]

On the Pershing Road location, environmental concerns had been potential deterrents for current and future ownership. If a potential buyer would be interested in the property, environmental site assessments would typically be required by the mortgage lending institution in order to protect its investment even though the assessments are not required by law, according to environmental scientist and higher education administrator, Dr. Elizabeth Kline.[25] Dr. Kline, who has completed hundreds of environmental site assessments on behalf of potential owners and banks, has found assessments that find potential hazards do not necessarily halt the purchase of properties. Liability forms can be completed so that the bank can be protected should anyone become ill or seek to sue the owner.

In 2017, a Voluntary Action Program (VAP) Phase I property assessment was completed on the Mosaic Tile site for the Zanesville Muskingum County Coalition.[26] The purpose of the assessment, as described in the report, was "to aid in potential future redevelopment of the Property."[27] The overall conclusion from the report indicated that "there is reason to suspect that a release of hazardous substances and/or petroleum product has or may have occurred on, is underlying, or is emanating from the Property."[28] A summary from the report included details concerning the evidence of Identified Areas (IAs) and Recognized Environmental Conditions (RECs) of the property and the significance of those. The conclusions include over a dozen IAs and RECs.[29] One example described was "the potential for environmental impact to the subsurface from the contents of former lagoons on the Property's western portion."[30] These lagoons were used to "store tile glaze for off-site disposal" by Mosaic but were later used by the Akro Corporation to store non-hazardous waste latex.[31]

Not only does the Pershing Road property have back taxes, an unpaid mortgage, and hazardous environmental issues, there is another associated property less than a mile away that had been used for a "dumpsite." The Mosaic Tile Company apparently used this site to dump wastes, glazes, and damaged tile products.[32] This site, approximately four acres, is surrounded by homes between the parallel roads of Benjamin Avenue and Woody Lane.[33] The property is across the road and to the southwest of the main Mosaic Tile property. (The "road" referenced here is Coopermill Road. Pershing and Coopermill Roads connect at the railroad tracks where the name changes from one to the other.) The dumpsite, as it is referred to in reports produced by the Environmental Protection Agency (EPA), had been abandoned until 1991, when families at that time living in the adjacent residences complained.[34] At least four children who may have played on the property were tested for lead poisoning.[35] Unfortunately, no news articles or EPA reports can be found with the results of those tests for the children. The Ohio EPA "confirmed the presence of high levels of lead in the soil and higher than normal levels in the air over the site."[36]

In 1991, the EPA identified the property owner was still Collins & Aikman. The company began the removal of the dangerous substances "until they declared bankruptcy."[37] At that point, the Collins & Aikman Corporation created a Custodial Trust to provide future resources for maintaining the property.[38] The EPA ordered the property to have some of the materials removed, other areas to be covered by various treatment solutions, and groundwater monitoring wells.[39] Additionally, the property was completely surrounded with a chain-link fence with locked gates and "no trespassing" signs posted.[40] The Ohio EPA conducted site monitoring checks of the groundwater for many years to ensure the property was properly maintained and that agency reported that the site had been used to dispose of manufacturing wastes by the Mosaic Tile Company.[41] Further, the Ohio EPA indicated that "many types of tiles were decorated with glazes there were either dipped or bushed [*sic*] onto the tiles. A common pigment in tile glazes was white lead, a mixture of lead carbonate and lead hydroxide."[42] While many other companies owned the property after Mosaic closed the factory, the Ohio EPA indicated that these "wastes may be the source of lead contamination in soils at the site."[43] Ramboll Environ's report indicated that the dumping of product at this location stopped in "mid–1967 when Mosaic Tile ceased operations in Zanesville."[44] The most recent available documentation for the dumpsite was from October 2019 which indicated that "there have been no changes in property conditions or use that could present an increased risk to occupants, workers, etc. through exposure to contamination on site."[45]

Mosaic Tile Company, dumpsite between Benjamin Avenue and Woody Lane.

Just prior to the Phase I assessment work, in 2016, the City of Zanesville had held "community visioning and planning sessions" to gather input for this site and other abandoned sites in the area.[46] One survey gathered responses of area residents and were categorized into leisure, emergency services, food, and shopping options. The most votes were for emergency services, followed by leisure (e.g., pools and sports). Shopping and food options closed out the top four.

In 2020, Zanesville Mayor Donald Mason identified his vision for the property while in his first year of his term. This term was Mason's third non-consecutive term having held this office for two terms from 1983 through 1991. With his mayoral experience and a variety of other prominent public service positions between those years and now, Mayor Mason indicated he wanted to build on the land's existing strengths.[47] He believed the strengths included the location near the Muskingum County Fairgrounds and the physical components of the structures that still existed on site. Mayor Mason shared his informal "SWOT" analysis by indicating that, while the site needed a lot of work, the remaining structures were solid. These buildings, built with double brick walls like old prisons, courthouses, and governmental buildings, were constructed to withstand decades of use. A weakness of the property was that the modern-day size of tractor-trailers would not easily navigate or access the residential roads leading to the property. The Mayor agreed that the worst threat to this property would be for nothing to be done, allowing it to rot and decay.[48]

In order to move forward, the city authorized a Phase II environmental site assessment to add to the information gained through the previously completed Phase I site information assessment report. If the current owner does not take a proactive approach, cleaning up or selling the property, the city could be left with a major eyesore, and potentially valuable but also potentially environmentally damaged land.

Mayor Mason indicated that the Auditor's office could act on the company's failure to pay the taxes. After that, the Muskingum County Land Reutilization Corporation, known commonly as the Land Bank, would obtain the property. The Land Bank's mission as a "quasi-governmental, non-profit corporation" is to "return land and vacant abandoned properties to a productive use; reduce blight, increase property values, support community land use goals; and improve the quality of life for all county residents."[49] Andy Roberts, Executive Director of the Land Bank, confirmed that the Land Bank had been reviewing the current situation with the property, including the on-going Phase II environmental review.[50] Hypothetically, once the property was within the control of the local governmental entities, the Mayor would have the City of Zanesville complete site plans and seek community input to determine a possible layout that could suit the neighborhood.

Mayor Mason saw the resolution of this property's blight as a major priority for his administration. As a lifelong resident of Zanesville, he recalled the beauty of the tiles in schools and public buildings and in his own home, which prior owners had covered with carpet or some other floor style of the day. He agreed that "we took this tile for granted."[51] With the Mayor's leadership, there could be hope yet that the history of the Mosaic Tile Company and its products will be remembered and respected moving forward.

8

Decorative and Practical Architectural Installations in Southeastern Ohio

The original vision of the Mosaic Tile Company's founders was to create beautiful mosaic murals with innovative tile production and installation. Many architectural beauties still are standing more than 50 years since the Zanesville factory closed, which is a testament to the durability of the company's products and practices. This chronological review of exterior and interior tile displays within Zanesville area buildings will be highlighted with illustrations of as many works as possible.

1894–1900

Built in the same year, two new schools for Zanesville area students were erected in 1896, Grant School and Garfield School. The growth of the Zanesville area in the late 1800s, especially in the newly established Brighton area and the annexed Putnam area, created the need for new buildings. According to Sutor, "the classes graduating from the high school had been increasing in numbers very rapidly...."[1] The importance of education in a time when many students did not continue beyond grammar school and the growth of the city's population led the school board to make the decision to spend funds to build two new schools. For $15,438 in 1896, Garfield, a four-room brick building, was constructed, and for $15,550, Grant, also a four-room brick building, was constructed.[2]

The two buildings had some similarities: Both schools had towers with turret roofs that flanked the buildings, towers over the middle of the buildings, tall windows, arched doorways, brick facades, and colorful tiles to adorn many of the architectural features. Mosaic tiles wrapped around the circular turrets just below the rounded roofs. Located on the corner of today's Brighton Boulevard and Dryden road, the tiles on Garfield's towers were decorated with blue and white florals, ovals, and leaves. Over the front door frame, the name of the school was made of capital letter tiles and framed with blue and white complementary tiles. In the center of the front façade, just below the middle "bell tower" feature, was a large circular tile display, called a roundel, which was created with brown, white, and dark blue tiles. Over the curved windows on the sides of the building were additional rectangular shaped frames of tiles made of browns, blues, and whites with a star-like design.

On McIntire Avenue in the Putnam area, the architectural feature under Grant's turrets were tiles with square features framing other tiles with curved designs in the middle section. Over the rear door of the building, more decorative tiles with shapes similar to fleur de lis and swirls were featured. Again, the school's name was posted similarly to Garfield's over the front door.

The Grant building was utilized as a school until the 1978–1979 school year, whereas Garfield was used until 1990 even while in terrible shape after a possible tornado or high wind damage.[3] Both buildings were deemed unusable but many efforts were made by

Garfield School, facing southwest toward Brighton Boulevard and Dryden Road (courtesy David M. Taylor)

Garfield School, turret (courtesy David M. Taylor).

different organizations to attempt to repair the damages. The cost may have been prohibitive, as indicated in 1997 by the owner at the time of Garfield, who was hoping to repurpose the building into an antique shop and community space.[4] The owner noted that the cost would be over $100,000 to repair the bell tower, which had been damaged in a storm and had crashed into the roof.[5] Garfield was demolished in 2001, leaving a grass-covered empty field.[6] Grant was demolished in 1987 and the land has been used for a playground for the southern Putnam neighborhood.[7] Unfortunately, the wrecking ball took down

Grant School, postcard.

St. Nicholas Catholic Church postcard, facing south toward Main Street.

everything, including the tiles. It would have been too costly for demolition crews to try to salvage the tiles, and at the time, the tiles may not have been appreciated for their local significance.

Commonly thought of as the very first installation of Mosaic's mural mosaic designs of a specific image, the St. Nicholas Catholic Church façade in Zanesville was finished in 1899. This church was not the first building for this congregation. Originally made up of German immigrants, the congregation had grown since the first church was completed in 1827.[8] The work on the new building began in 1898 and was described as a Romanesque style, similar to St. Peter's of Rome.[9] The church is an "80 by 110-foot structure of mottled brick with terra cotta trimmings and a large dome."[10] Herman Mueller began his design of the semi-circular mosaic of Christopher Columbus's landing. This mural was positioned above the front door of the church facing the intersection of Main and Ninth Streets. The scene is of Christopher Columbus standing among his shipmates and the indigenous people of the Americas. Also depicted is a priest, who is the conveyor of the Christian message. In the background is the horizon of the ocean and Columbus's fleet of ships. The Purviances' resource indicated that this mural was an adaptation of a painting in the United States Capitol Rotunda.[11] If this is the case, then likely the painting was the *Landing of Columbus*, an oil on canvas by John Vanderlyn and installed in the Rotunda in January 1847.[12] The St. Nicholas Church's Columbus scene is surrounded by a buff stone archway that separates the mural from the brick exterior wall. Hovering over the archway are two angel images dressed in blue flowing robes, white wings, and

St. Nicholas Catholic Church: mural and angels above entry.

St. Nicholas Catholic Church: Mosaic Tile Company advertisement circa 1900 (courtesy Delbert Tullius, Jr.)

blowing trumpets—all made in the mosaic method within a field of reddish-brown tiles on opposite sides and looking down upon the Columbus scene.

To the right of the doorway is a small rectangular tile space with the date of the building completion, 1899, made of tiles. According to Schneider's account on the church's website, the floors of the vestibules and sanctuary are tiled as well.[13] The community is blessed to still have this wonderful building.

1900–1920

Albert P. Rogge, the 16-year-old son of Henry Rogge, continued the management of his late father's hotel with a popular restaurant in downtown Zanesville, positioned on the street near a bustling passenger train railroad stop.[14] With growing demand from those traveling the railroad in 1900, Albert added a four-story brick hotel to his property and included "new" technology and conveniences of "elevators, steam heat, electric lights, hot and cold water and a complete telephone system."[15] To add to the Hotel Rogge's décor, Albert contracted with the Mosaic Tile Company to install a fireplace mantel and surround with mosaic tile designs of flowers and the coat of arms for the Rogge family.[16] According to the *Times Recorder* in 1899, the Mosaic Tile Company was "awarded the contract for the floor work of the new Hotel Rogge."[17] The floor in this area, the west

ROGGE HOTEL, ZANESVILLE, OHIO.

Hotel Rogge postcard, postmarked 1935.

end of the lobby, was also a decorative tile display with nearly 3,000 square feet of "tile blended in the most beautiful colors and designs."[18] After about 70 years of use as a hotel and eventually a home for senior citizens, the building did not pass fire marshal inspections and had to be boarded up, as the repairs were too expensive. Eventually demolished in 1974, the hotel, including the tile work, was lost to history.[19]

Known as the "County Poor House" when built in 1840, this public home provided for those in need with a residence and an opportunity to work on the House's farm.[20] With a name change to the County Infirmary in 1850, the county constructed a larger facility in 1880 on the property.[21] In 1900, the building

Hotel Rogge fireplace (courtesy Muskingum County History)

Adena Court Apartments patio.

underwent remodeling, and Mosaic Tile was contracted to provide the flooring in the main hall and bathrooms.[22] The building continued to serve low income senior citizens until the building was condemned and eventually transferred to Zane State College in 2010, after which the building was demolished after asbestos abatement had been completed.

What is now commonly referred to as the Adena Court Apartments was originally a three-story mansion built for Dr. Charles Lenhart between 1906 and 1907 as his residence and office.[23] The larger building, adding to a smaller brick original building on the property, is supported by oversized

Adena Court Apartments entry.

sandstone blocks. Noted in newspaper accounts, the style of the architecture is Colonial Revival and is a "buff brick building trimmed in smooth-faced limestone ... beautiful arches and balconies on its first two stories. Above the third story is an ornate modeled metal cornice."[24] The patio, surrounded by sandstone blocks, is an entryway of Mosaic Tile paving tiles; the tiles have a gray and white circular design pattern and cover the entire front area leading to the building. The building was added to the National Register of Historic Places in 1990 and is still in use as private apartments.[25]

Originally known as the senior high school, the Lash High School building was opened for education in January of 1908.[26] Located on space that was "bounded by North Fifth and Sixth streets and Elberon avenue," the building was touted as being large enough and well-equipped to educate generations of Zanesville students.[27] That did not actually happen, though, as an addition to the Lash building and then eventually a brand new high school would be built within just a few decades. The building was designed as a modified English collegiate with "chocolate colored brick walls" and the interior floors, 8,000 feet total, were covered by Mosaic Tile products.[28] This building was vacated as a high school and used for other purposes, but eventually was torn down in 1986.[29]

The building of the Young Men's Christian Association (YMCA) began with a unique cornerstone laying event featuring the cornerstone made of Mosaic Tile in 1919.[30] This laying of tile was just the beginning of Mosaic's involvement in this building. The ground-breaking ceremony was led by two individuals, one of whom was William Shinnick, general manager of Mosaic Tile, who also had been one of the two largest contributors to the YMCA's building campaign.[31] Within the building, Mosaic Tile Company products, along with American Encaustic Tiling Company material, was used for the floors of the

Lash High School postcard, postmarked 1920.

Y. M. C. A., ZANESVILLE, OHIO.

YMCA postcard.

building and the addition of a swimming pool in 1922.[32] The company continued to be involved in upgrades in activities for the young children who attended the YMCA. "Teen Tyme" was a room within the building dedicated to the students, and Mosaic Tile was contracted by the Rotary Club of Zanesville to add a new tile shuffleboard floor to this room in 1951.[33] One of the popular games of the time, shuffleboard was noted as a "permanent fixture" in many facilities like the YMCAs across the nation.[34] This "weatherproof ceramic Mosaic tile, with all-tile numerals and markers, provide a smooth glass-like surface for the players ... [and] are unaffected by freeze or thaw, and furnish fun for many a generation."[35]

1920–1950

In 1926, the Peoples Savings Bank remodeled and doubled the previously used space of shops for their newly reopened building on North Fourth Street of downtown Zanesville.[36] The bank featured new tile floors manufactured by the Mosaic Tile Company. Photos of this building have been included in Sims' and Lynch's book featuring the history of Zanesville, though the building no longer stands on North Fourth Street.[37]

The Mosaic Tile Company designed and installed the large mural within the lobby of the Municipal Auditorium, referred to as the "tile mural of pioneer Zanesville," in 1940.[38] The auditorium was funded as part of the Works Progress Administration (WPA), a federally funded employment program created by President Franklin Roosevelt.[39] The Auditorium was intended to serve the community with options for school plays, basketball games, workshops, and theater productions. Mosaic Tile products were used extensively throughout the building with 47,000 pieces totaling 13,000 square feet.[40] The featured work is the tile mural in the auditorium's lobby designed by Mosaic Tile's assistant artistic director, Byron Shrider.[41] The scene, measuring 8 feet by 10 feet, is a tile collage featuring the image of Ebenezer Zane in buckskin garb holding a gun and pointing the way to the new land in the west. Near Zane is General Rufus Putnam, who led the pioneers to the Northwest Territory and established Marietta. Also represented is an Indigenous American who represents the tribes that lived in this part of Ohio, such as the Delawares, Wyandots, Shawnee, and Seneca.[42] Slaves were poorly portrayed with unfortunate stereotypical features and presumably are depicted escaping the south through the Underground Railroad, of which several stations were located in Muskingum County. The Municipal Auditorium was renamed Secrest Auditorium in honor of State Representative Robert T. Secrest when renovations were completed in 1987.[43] The facility currently provides a venue for local and national theatrical performances and special events.

Another remodeling of a store during this time period was that of the Williams Bakery and Delicatessen on Market Street in 1947.[44] Williams Bakery, originally built in

Secrest Auditorium mural in foyer (courtesy Secrest Auditorium and the City of Zanesville).

1932, had exterior tiles and large glass windows installed on the front of the store. This added "twice the space" that it had originally.[45] The business was eager to serve its customers in the late 1940s and continued its service for decades. This building is still in place, although empty for now, and the exterior tile can be seen, although some of the tile façade seems to have been painted and is peeling.

The Commercial Supply, Inc., was an office supply store located at the corner of Fourth and Market Streets. The new store opened in November 1947 after remodeling the existing building. The local paper indicated that the building boasted a new entry

Secrest Auditorium flooring and mural (courtesy Secrest Auditorium and the City of Zanesville)

Secrest Auditorium postcard.

Williams Bakery front entry.

with plate glass windows and a "monogrammed tile entrance, especially designed by the Mosaic Tile Company."[46]

1950–1960

A beautiful new church on Seventh Street was built for the St. John's Lutheran Church congregation in 1927.[47] The design of this building, intended to seat 650 people, was a "pure Gothic architecture built of mingled shades of brick trimmed with art stone."[48] Over two decades later, the congregation needed more space to worship and, thanks to the generosity of several families, the church built the Parish Hall building which also included the Baker Chapel in 1950.[49] This chapel was funded by the family of Albert T. Baker, a long-time member and church leader. Under the beautiful stained-glass windows at the front of the chapel, the tiles in the Baker Chapel span the wainscoting on the wall, the altar, the floor, and the stairs. Bright blue and yellow tile frame the images of the "praying cherubim, symbolic of worship" on the altar.[50] The cherubim are approximately three feet in height and made of a mosaic mixture of an angel dressed in white and burgundy robes with yellow wings and a halo of light. Atop the altar is the "throne" embellished with a burgundy and yellow "I H S" (the first three letters of the Greek name of Jesus) surrounded with yellow tile symbolizing the name Jesus Christ.[51] The floor tiles also contain symbols for the Lutheran tradition: "seals of the four evangelists interspersed by Luther's coat-of-arms inserted in face of the altar steps. Also found on the steps are symbols of the pelican, the Book and candlesticks, the victorious Lamb, the 'Chi Rho' and the keys."[52] The congregation of St. John's Lutheran Church can continue to enjoy the Baker Chapel for many years to come.

Part of a 1951 renovation of the exterior of the Ohio Fuel Gas Company's building on Fourth Street featured Mosaic Tile's black and yellow tiles.[53] Now home to the Stubbins, Watson, Bryan and Witucky law firm, the original Ohio Fuel Gas name and the image of a flickering flame have been changed or covered to display the current company name and street address.

In the need for a new building, an automotive parts store, Morris and Snyder Tires, was constructed on Linden Avenue just north of the Y-Bridge in 1959. The newspaper announcement of this new venture described that the one-story concrete building had Mosaic Tile panels on the front and side of the entry.[54] The panels featured automotive and transportation images, designed by Byron Shrider, to tie into Morris & Snyder's target market.[55] While the building still exists, the tile is either gone or hidden by rectangular metal tin.

An exciting new feature for Zanesville Country Club members was a swimming pool added in 1953.[56] The construction contract was given to Dunzweiler Construction Company which worked on many Zanesville area facilities.[57] This pool was funded primarily by the members of the Club and the final cost was estimated at $45,000. The pool measured 30 by 75 feet, with a 10-foot walkway around the pool that was completed with Mosaic Tile products. Also, the "scum gutters and portions of the wainscoting" were Mosaic Tile.[58] This pool was enjoyed by the members and guests of the Country Club until 1998, when it was replaced.

J.C. Penney was a featured shopping destination in Zanesville's downtown, starting with the first store built in 1923.[59] The chain built a new "modern" store in 1953, a

Baker Chapel in St. John's Lutheran Church (courtesy W. Norman Shade, St. John's Lutheran Church).

two-story building with the "latest in store planning, designed for the convenience and comfort of the shopper and presenting up-to-the minute merchandise in the most modern and attractive manner."[60] This modern facility featured 2,712 square feet of "three-quarter inch ceramic"; the tile was used for the exterior store front, in the vestibule, and in restrooms.[61] Widely believed to be a major loss to what used to be a thriving downtown economic center over a 30-year period, J.C. Penney vacated the North Fifth Street downtown building in 1980 and moved into an anchor space in the shopping mall that was built on the northern end of Maple Avenue, north of downtown.[62] The building structure has remained at the Fifth Street location but has undergone major renovations for various county offices.

Morris and Snyder Tires (courtesy Muskingum County History).

Zanesville Country Club postcard.

Built in 1954, a brand-new building for the Zanesville Federal Savings & Loan Association used the Granitex brand of tile by the Mosaic Tile Company in the lobby of the building.[63] Over the years, after a few different occupants, the new owners, Quality Care Partners (QCP), remodeled but left several homages to the era of the '50s. It appears that the entryway's tile floor is still the "rich, earthly color-mottled tile" that Mosaic advertised.[64] However, a surprise on the author's visit were two massive mural paintings by Alean Galigher, as mentioned in a local newspaper article, hung on the walls of the interior offices. QCP's Public Relation Marketing Specialist Jennifer Martin indicated that these were original to the 1954 building along with the immense vault.[65] The first of the two murals by Galigher was focused on the pioneers of the area with familiar images likely of Ebenezer Zane and John McIntire along with local features of the Headley Inn (one of the first inns on the National Road, built in 1833 to 1835), the Lorena sternwheeler of 1895, and the covered Y-Bridge of 1832.[66] The second mural is focused on local industry, with tile as one of the primary images. Stereotypical of the 1950s, men are shown with the heavy-lifting jobs, and women are busy with the color and design work. The time seems to span from the late 1800s to the mid–1900s. Though the paintings are not Mosaic Tile work, these do represent the tile industry's rich history in the area.

As mentioned earlier, the Zanesville City Schools had built Lash High School in 1908; it was to serve students for generations. The actual growth of the schools demanded another larger building in the 1950s. Using the 65-acre property previously occupied by the John McIntire Children's Home, this new five-level, $4 million building was the city school district's fourth high school. Opening in the fall of 1954, the school featured many areas of Mosaic Tile on the interior: Floors, walls, drinking fountain surrounds, gymnasium locker rooms and showers, and in the lobby.[67] On the exterior of the building facing Blue Avenue, large decorative blocks of colorful tile were installed: The "three large mosaic blocks are fitted on

Quality Care Partners entryway (courtesy Jennifer Martin).

Quality Care Partners industry painting (courtesy Jennifer Martin).

Quality Care Partners transportation painting (courtesy Jennifer Martin).

Zanesville High School postcard.

the east side of the structure to blend in with the color scheme of the building."[68] This high school lasted nearly 55 years, but became outdated and too small for the class sizes, and a new school was built on the same property. The 1954 building was demolished in 2010.[69]

In 1955, Mosaic Tile worked with the First Trust & Savings Bank to remodel their existing building at 434 Main Street. This "modernization" included "old tellers' cages" being replaced with tiled counters along with a new tile floor.[70] This building was in use until the mid–1970s when the entire building was demolished to make way for a new and bigger bank building.[71]

Zanesville had the benefit of two large hospitals since the 1890s, including the Good Samaritan Hospital on Forrest Avenue. One of the several renovations to that site included a seven story addition in 1956.[72] Within a congratulatory newspaper advertisement for the opening of the Good Samaritan addition, the Mosaic Tile Company told of the products that were used.[73] This included the "Impervious Electrically Conductive Ceramic" tile to reduce the "danger of anesthesia explosion due to electrostatic spark discharge or electrical shock."[74] Tile was installed in at least one operating room, a kitchen, and a "scrub-up" room on both the floors and walls.[75] When the two hospitals, Good Samaritan and Bethesda, merged in 1997, a plan was put into motion to scale down to only one larger hospital in Zanesville, and the Good Samaritan building was demolished in 2016.[76]

Merging newspapers, the *Zanesville Signal* and the *Times Recorder*, required a new building and more modern machinery. In 1926, this new building opened on Fourth Street and produced the first combined newspaper in September of that year.[77] This building worked effectively until the newspaper needed more space. In 1958 the exterior of the addition on the west side of the building was seemingly a blank canvas for a Mosaic Tile mural scene.[78] According to Roy E. Greene's obituary, he was the designer of the mural which was described by the *Times Recorder* as images of "several phases of newspaper production starting with the photographer and the editor in the middle … the linotype operator in the left (bottom), stereotype plates from which the type is printed on the blank paper, a hand compositor preparing type in the upper left, a roll of newsprint feeding into a press and the printed paper coming out at the top right and ending with the carrier boy at the bottom right."[79] A newspaper tells a story and so does this Mosaic Tile work. The newspaper is no longer the owner of the building, but the building is still enjoyable today; still enjoyable today; it is now occupied by the City of Zanesville with space for the Public Safety department.[80]

In the 1950s the First Evangelical United Brethren Church had outgrown its downtown location and sought a new space for its expanding congregation. Seeing the future growth of the area near the new Zanesville High School building and buying the property across the street from the planned high school in 1953, this church was the newest neighbor at the corner of Blue Avenue and Fairmont Street.[81] Designed as a semi–Gothic style, Sigman & Tribble Architects drew the plans and the construction company was Dunzweiler Construction of Zanesville.[82] The building specifications called for "nothing less than perfect tile work," identified the wall tile as Mosaic Tile's Harmonitone wall tile, and indicated that quarry tile floors would be Mosaic Tile Company's as well.[83] The construction began in 1958 and the final dedication event was on September 27, 1959. Specified in the details for products to be used in this project, Mosaic Tile played a major part in restrooms, kitchen, and the large open fellowship hall. The Evangelical United Brethren Church and the Methodist Church merged in 1968 and the name of this church was

Times Recorder building facing south toward Fourth Street.

changed to Faith United Methodist Church.[84] Still in great condition, the tiles throughout the church have been manufactured to last for decades.

Another large-scale project was the Dillon Dam control tower in the north-western part of Muskingum County in 1960. The leaders of the region organized the Muskingum River Watershed Conservancy District in response to the Great Flood of

Faith United Methodist Church restroom.

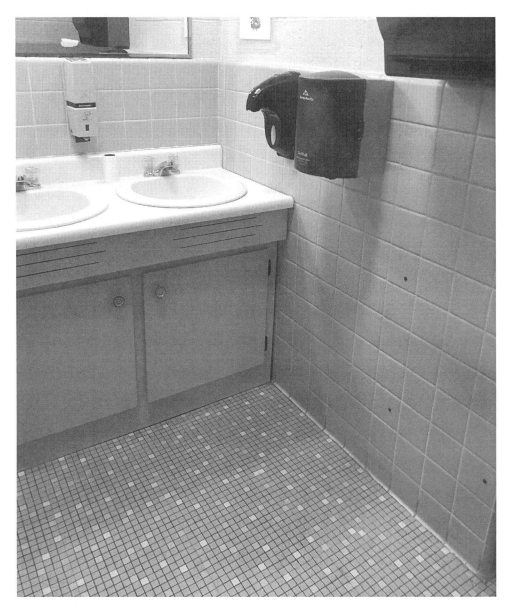

Faith United Methodist Church restroom.

1913 to "construct dams and reservoirs to reduce the effects of potential flooding and capture the floodwaters for beneficial public uses."[85] The $31 million project culminated in
1960, with 15 dams constructed in the District.[86] Although the dams and reservoirs could
not guarantee that flooding would never happen again, they wanted to reduce the potential damage of flooding in the future. Mosaic Tile's involvement was the production of
numerical tiles on the façade of the Control Tower which would visually show the height
of the rising waters. At the base of the tower, the numbers begin at 752 feet going up to
815 feet. The tower itself is much taller than the top of the numerical tiles. The company
sponsored a congratulatory advertisement called "a sermon written on the face of the
land"[87] that detailed the 33-year battle to finish the district's work on flood control. The

Faith United Methodist Church facing southeast toward Blue Avenue and Fairmont Street.

ad ended with: "We look upon the dedication of Dillon Dam as representing one of the most far-reaching strides in the advancement of our community and, in fact, in the progress of the Nation."[88]

On a tangential note related to the various construction jobs in Zanesville and involving the Mosaic Tile Company, local hearsay claims that when a large project was nearly completed and holes needed to be filled for landscaping, parking lots, or pathways the construction company would use broken bits of tiles to fill those vast spaces. A friend had mentioned to me that when she has worked in her yard to plant flowers, she would often dig up small fragments of tiles. While communicating with a relative of the Dunzweiler Construction Company, Bruce C. Dunzweiler, he also mentioned that this would often occur, and he specifically knew that this was how the parking lot of Faith United Methodist Church was completed. The hearsay was confirmed with evidence when lights were installed at a local school, and the ground had been dug up to run the wiring. When the wiring was covered up with the displaced soil, hundreds of bits of Mosaic Tile—with the racetrack oval clearly marked on some of the pieces—were mixed into and on top of the dirt. These locations—my friend's yard, Faith UMC's parking lot, and the school's lighting—are all within a mile of each other. Perhaps this, at the time, was a useful recycling of broken tiles that were not meant to be sold.

Dillon Dam Control Tower building and catwalk.

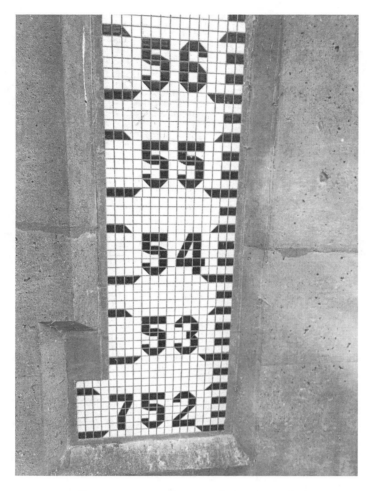

Dillon Dam Control Tower, tile height marker.

Dates Unknown and Connections Unconfirmed

Over the years, stories have run rampant with claims that the Mosaic Tile Company was involved in the installation of tiles on interior and exterior features of various Zanesville area buildings. Those stories were local folklore that cannot be confirmed through books or newspaper articles, but memories of residents are strong and sentimental. This section will review some tile work that could possibly be Mosaic Tile's but is not confirmed in records. We can all learn from documenting our past, or the lack thereof, as we move forward in the 21st century and reminisce about the 19th and 20th centuries.

As customers stepped out of their buggies, railcars, or new automobiles, they would enter the storefronts of Zanesville's early department and specialty stores (i.e., long before malls and online shopping). Decorative entryways seemed to be all the rage in the early 1900s and Mosaic Tile may have been very involved in the installations of these. One example, a long-time favorite of Zanesville residents, the Bloomer Candy Company in downtown Zanesville enjoyed a long run on Third Street.[89] The company began in 1879 and established stores downtown as early as 1896. At some point, the Bloomer's building was outfitted with a decorative tile entrance customized with the name of the company in

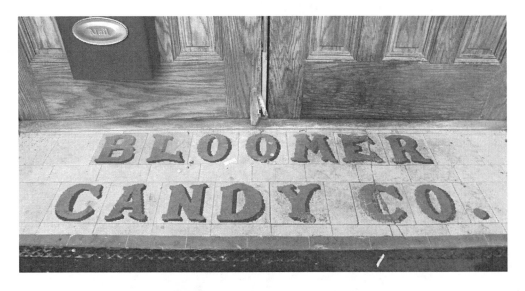

Bloomer's Candy entryway (courtesy David M. Taylor).

capital letters in green with a black outline. Unfortunately, Bloomer's left the downtown area and moved around the Zanesville area before relocating completely to Columbus. This building and its beautiful entryway were demolished in 2014.

Clossman Hardware was originally built in 1876, and its building has been listed on the National Register of Historic Places.[90] In 1922, the building was remodeled and that likely was when the exterior tiles were installed. Along the base of the building, under the large windows, on both sides of the double doorway are black square tiles with inset green tiles which are turned 45 degrees as accent pieces. The entryway, reminiscent of the Bloomer Candy Company entryway, has a base of tan square tiles and a featured rectangular space for the name of the building "Clossman Hardware Co" and the phrase "Since 1876." The letters and numbers are one-inch black tiles. This building housed the hardware store until the middle 1990s, when the building was sold and re-opened in 1997 as Clossman's Antiques Market. Today, with new owners, the Clossman Unique Market is eager to display historical artifacts about the building along with their stock of "over 8000 sq ft of new, antique and vintage curiosities of a huge variety."[91] The owners, James and Allison Campsey, also bring their expertise with rocks, crystals, and metaphysical products and operate Gemini's Eclectic Emporium within the Market.[92] Even though the company that produced the tiles cannot yet be identified, the Campseys are happy that the tiles were likely produced locally and are eager to welcome visitors to the downtown shopping area.

A neighbor to Clossman's is the building housing the Zanesville Appalachian Arts Project (ZAAP). This building was constructed in 1900 and has had many owners and occupants over the past 120 years. The current owner, Paul Emory, is a lifetime Zanesville area resident and talented artist who has a passion for buying and restoring buildings in downtown Zanesville that would otherwise meet the wrecking ball.[93] The ZAAP building, remodeled by Emory in 1999, is filled with its original tiles inside and out. The first floor has gorgeous small ivory, black, and deep red tiles creating intricate lined rows, diamond shapes, and interconnected borders throughout. Leading into the building, the long entryway, likely installed when first built, is a basketweave design of tiles in rectangular browns, tans, grays, and small square black tiles.

Clossman Unique Market entryway (courtesy James M. Campsey, Jr.).

On the same side of the street, The Wood Shop, occupies the next building with a very distinctive entryway. This building, constructed in the early 1900s, housed the Art Coyle Men's Shop from 1929 to the late 1950s.[94] The entryway gave permanent signage for Art Coyle. Along the wall under the windows are 4-inch light green tiles spanning most of the length with smaller white and green tiles inserted to spell "ART COYLE" on both sides of the entry. Additionally, the walkway has multiple tiles of white, green, and golden yellow creating a repeating geometric design. Again, inset into the background of the design are white with green tiles spelling the company name. Paul Emory, also owner of this building, wanted to save this building and, in doing so, has saved a beautiful storefront.

Diagonally across Main Street is a currently unoccupied building that most recently housed an antique store. The amazing tile work on the entry of this building cannot be overlooked, even if not confirmed. Longtime Zanesville residents fondly remember the Nader's department store. By tracing the company's location in the *City Directory*, it appears that the store had multiple locations from the early 1900s through its closing in the late 1990s.[95] Beginning in 1910, one of the locations of the company was at 610 Main Street and by 1912, the company expanded into the 616 Main Street building.[96] Comparing old photos of the Nader's stores and the current store at 616 Main, there are incredible differences, but what remains is the entryway. Under the large glass windows along the wall, light green, gray, and black tiles are randomly positioned, but some of these tiles have raised relief designs. Some designs appear to be florals and perhaps small fruits, but this is difficult to determine. From there, the doorway has small white, gray, and green

Zanesville Appalachian Arts Project entryway (courtesy Paul Emory).

Zanesville Appalachian Arts Project interior first floor (courtesy Paul Emory).

The Wood Shop entryway, formerly Art Coyle (courtesy Paul Emory).

Nader's entryway.

tiles randomly placed on the field and inserted in the middle is a script version of the name Nader's with the address of 616 Main Street incorporated into the name's design. This company moved to another location downtown on Market Street in 1938.[97]

South of these Main Street stores is another building, also on the U.S. National Register of Historic Places: the Black-Elliott Block building, constructed in 1876. Built for two entrepreneurs, Henry Elliott and Peter Black, the three-story Italianate style building allowed Black and Elliott to each have a side of the building to sell their wares.[98] Over the years, the building underwent renovations to the façade and housed a variety of businesses including SS Kresge, the Jupiter Discount Store, and, today, the Olde Towne Antique Mall. Owner Jeffrey Snyder shared that the entryway has no documented proof that is connected to Mosaic but agreed that it does indeed appear to be similar to other tile work on entries in the downtown area.[99] Unfortunately, the entryway is also missing the name of the company that was housed in the building at the time and probably had commissioned the tile. What remains is a field of small tiles in varying shades of brown with a border of dark green tiles around the perimeter. While visiting the store, Mr. Snyder shared several unique Mosaic Tile products which will be highlighted in an upcoming chapter.

Away from Main Street, just a few blocks to the west, is a brick building with the trademark Coca-Cola name in tile on the façade. Though the work could have been installed earlier, in 1960, the Coca-Cola Company was featured in a newspaper article with a photo of the building facing Seventh Street with the tile display of the company's brand name.[100] The building was constructed in 1937 and served as a "production and

Antique Mall entryway (courtesy Jeffrey Snyder).

distribution facility until 1986."[101] While this cannot be confirmed as a Mosaic Tile product, it is commonly thought to be. Karlson had included a photo of this tile work in his book in 1998 in the Mosaic Tile section; however, he did not add any narrative about the photo.[102] According to a blogsite focused on multiple Coca-Cola buildings, the author indicates that the "tile is original to the building" and since this building is located in the "Clay City ... this tile panel seems to be a unique alternative to Coca-Cola's standard use of terra cotta."[103] Located over the first-floor windows, the red base tiles make the brand name in white tile stand out. Two accent images of Coke bottles are on either end and the whole display is surrounded with white tiles and green corner tiles.

Spanning north to south from Fifth to Fourth Streets and bordered by Market Street, the Zanesville City Hall has multiple entries that should be examined. This building ties into the long tradition of a local farmer's market reaching into the early 1800s and in Zanesville a market house served as the place for farmers to gather weekly for area residents to purchase fresh produce.[104] Zanesville had an indoor market house, built in 1814.[105] This structure lasted only until 1827, while the second was built in 1832 and was demolished in 1863.[106] The third building lasted from 1864 to 1912, lost due to a fire. For a fourth building, in 1919, voters determined that tax dollars should be used for this one.[107] The new building was intended to serve as a combination market house and City Hall, and still remains as Zanesville's City Hall.[108] While the purpose and function of the building changed multiple times in the 20th century, the present-day City Hall still boasts tile work on the floors and entryways. This tile spans the side walls to the left and right of the entry doors and is in a random pattern with white, gray, browns, and brick red small tiles.

Coca-Cola façade facing Third Street.

Unfortunately, the tile cannot be confirmed as Mosaic Tile, though some residents think it may be.

Moving west along Fourth Street, near the *Times Recorder* building and the Adena Apartments is an abandoned four-story building that at one time housed the Montgomery Ward store. Built in 1925, the building was first used for a company which manufactured "work clothes."[109] Montgomery Ward opened the store in 1928 and was in operation until 1976.[110] The tile on this entryway covered a large space with large white and gray tiles placed in a checkerboard pattern. Bordering the tiles is an intricate pattern of smaller dark gray and white tiles. There are what appears to be black tiles along the wall under the windows but they could have been painted at some point. The building remains with windows boarded, but new ownership may lead to renovation of this beautiful brick building.

Tracing the location of the White Chevrolet automobile dealership has been quite the task, as the business occupied different locations downtown until it settled just off the west end of the Y-Bridge on West Main Street. Following the company name in the Zanesville City Directory helped to establish that Hugh White opened an automobile business in 1924 on Fifth Street.[111] The next edition of the City Directory indicated that the White Chevrolet Company was located on South Third Street.[112] Two years later in the 1928–1929 edition, the company was listed at 21 West Main Street.[113] Why is this tracing of the location important? It helps to figure out when the last remaining piece of the old Chevy business was installed within the sidewalk of West Main. This feature is just a few feet from the Y-Bridge and is easily missed when driving through the area. Approximately five feet across and just over two feet from top to bottom, a rectangular border

Zanesville City Hall facing Fourth Street.

Montgomery Ward building facing Fourth Street.

White Chevrolet sidewalk along West Main Street.

of brown tiles, most of which are less than an inch square, surrounds a field of yellow tiles and within the field is the bright blue and white logo of Chevrolet. While there is no record of the Mosaic Tile Company installing a custom sidewalk feature, thankfully that beauty remains.

While not in the downtown area, this home's front porch on Brighton Boulevard is only a few blocks away from the Mosaic Tile Company factory. Built in 1902, the home has a 15 by 15-foot porch surrounded by low walls and an overhanging roof. Unfortunately, no records exist to confirm the manufacturer, so it is only a possibility that the original builder of this home used Mosaic Tile products. A beautiful mix of mauve,

Front porch on Brighton Boulevard home (courtesy Joel Isaacson).

cream, green, blue one-inch tiles create a swirl pattern in the corners of the patio. In the center, the mauve tiles complete the full field of the patio. Still in great condition, this patio has very few missing tiles. Inside the house, two fireplaces have tile surrounds, which appear to be American Encaustic Tiling Company based on similar tiles found by the author. It is possible that both the patio and the fireplace surrounds are made by the same company, but it is a mystery given the location of the home.

There are several other buildings in downtown Zanesville and around Muskingum County that catch the eye, and we wonder about the tiles that can be seen. The provenance of the tile for these buildings will remain a mystery for now and while newspaper articles, books, and online resources did not provide answers, perhaps one day another source will supply confirmation.

Geometric shapes—multicolor tiles.

Geometric shape—multicolor tiles.

Top row: Floral tiles; bottom row: tea pot tiles (4 × 4 inch).

Patriot/minuteman tiles (4 × 9 inch and 6 × 6 inch).

Vintage style various scenes in brown, yellow (6 × 6 inch and 4 × 4 inch).

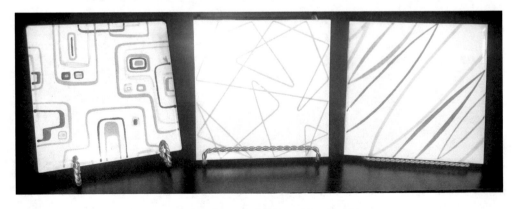

Retro style lines and shapes (6 × 6 inch).

Transportation-oriented scenes: two vintage cars and one horse (6 × 6 inch).

Florals in multicolors (6 × 6 inch).

Periwinkle blue images of sailboat and basket with leaves (4 × 4 inch).

Florals in multicolors (6 × 6 inch).

Florals in multicolors (6 × 6 inch).

Location scenes in brown (left to right): Model of early Pilgrim House, Plymouth, Massachusetts; Belle steamboat; California Union Insurance Company.

Location scenes in brown (left to right): Ballston Spa; the Clock Tower, Columbus, Mississippi; First Presbyterian Church, Beacon, New York.

Location scenes in brown (left to right): Chatham Light, Chatham, Massachusetts; Barbourville, Kentucky; Thunder Hole, Acadia National Park, Bar Harbor, Maine.

Location scenes in brown (left to right): Battle Monument, Bennington, Vermont; First Reformed Church, Boonton, New Jersey.

Location scenes in brown (left to right): Gem of the Adirondacks, Star Lake, New York; church with steeple; St. Cecilia's Church, Springdale, Connecticut.

Location scenes in brown (left to right): Windmill; covered bridge; map of the Kennebunks, Maine; blue and yellow house and couple strolling.

Multicolor fruit arrangement (4 × 4 inch tile; 6 × 6 inch tile).

Hexagonal tiles: rose image and plain gray.

Octagonal tile with racetrack oval logo in blue.

Delft-style tiles with windmill (4 × 4 inch) and sailboat (6 × 6 inch).

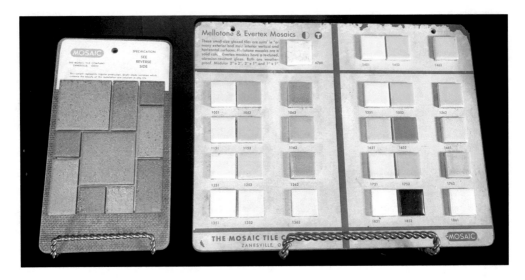

Sales samples.

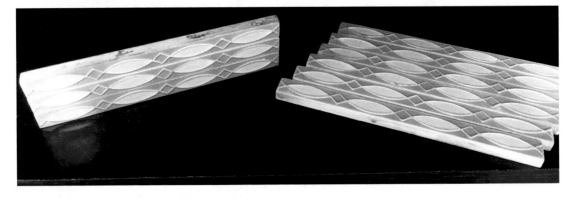

Border strip tiles with connecting oval shapes.

9

On the Road with Mosaic Tile—
Installations Within Ohio
and the United States

In addition to the showcase of work in the Zanesville area, the Mosaic Tile Company was contracted to create magnificent tile work throughout the state and the nation. This chapter focuses on interior and exterior designs confirmed to be the work of Mosaic Tile Company. Again, some are historical and no longer in place, while others survive to this day.

Ohio

On the Muskingum River, a series of locks and canals were constructed between 1836 and 1841 to help make the river navigable from Dresden to Marietta, bringing boats south to the Ohio River.[1] In the early days of this system, houses were built near some of the locks, so that a lockmaster, or locktender, could be easily summoned to open the locks and allow the boat to safely move through the canal.[2] The U.S. Engineer Office solicited proposals for building a lockmaster's house at Marietta, built in 1899 along the bank of the Muskingum River, near the Ohio River.[3] Over the front entryway porch, a Mosaic Tile composite featured the Great Seal of the United States with a large bald eagle with shield, holding arrows with its talons and olive branches in the other, along with 13 stars in a circular shape above the eagle's head. (This Great Seal tile composite was also installed in a Washington, D.C., building to be discussed later in this chapter.) Around the building, just below the roof soffit is a row of tiles in circular design, and between the first and second floor windows is a band of tiles in a design that has one row of angular ovals and another larger row of swirls, florals, and leaf shapes. On the side of the building that has a window for a third story, there is a collection of tiles surrounding that window that are round and floral in style. How do we know it is of the Mosaic Tile Company? The adhesive used to attach the tile had been exposed when one of the tiles fell off and the intertwined MTC mark was revealed. Still standing, the building has a historical marker on Front Street in downtown Marietta.

Just a few miles up the river from Marietta, or north on State Route 60, the town of Devola also is included in the lock and canal system on the Muskingum River. A similar tile display of the Great Seal of the United States ornamented the front gable of this now demolished locktender's house.[4] However, another possible Mosaic Tile

Lockmaster's House, Marietta Ohio.

Lockmaster's House, Great Seal of the United States.

Lockmaster's House, tile details.

Company installation remains at the lock in the form of tile numbers measuring the water level in the lock. These tiles look very similar to the Dillon Dam control tower numbers.

Previously described with its leadership in the building of the Dillon Dam, the Muskingum Watershed Conservancy District celebrated its 25th year with a large banquet in 1958.[5] Unveiled during that dinner, a large wall mural of tiles was designed to look like needlework and consisted of multiple images related to the work of the District. Some of the images represent a person with a fishing pole hooking a fish, two people sawing a tree, waterways, a hiker, trees, and agricultural farming scenes. This was an 8 by 15-foot Mosaic Tile mural for the District's offices in New Philadelphia.[6] This mural was reproduced in a 6 by 9-inch tile for souvenir and collection purposes (to be reviewed in a later chapter). District staff, Karen Miller, confirmed that when the District offices were remodeled the mural was dismantled.[7]

According to the program for the dedication event of the Noble County Courthouse in Caldwell, Mosaic Tile was one of tile companies which "furnished materials for the construction of the New Court House."[8] Many local products were used in its construction in 1934 with a unique building designed in a square so that "each office could have a window."[9] The construction workers were employed under the Civil Works Administration, a federal program to employ the unemployed during the Great Depression.[10]

Though records of this work have not been found, the Cincinnati Pearl Street market house, built in 1898, included a decorative panel by the Mosaic Tile Company.[11] The architect in charge of the Cincinnati construction, Harvey A. Hannaford, visited Zanesville to review the progress being made on the panel at the factory; the panel had been designed by Herman C. Mueller, co-founder of the company. Billed as "one of the best architects in the country," Mr. Hannaford praised the work and was "very liberal in his praise of the work and commended its artistic conception very highly."[12]

Along with many of Mosaic's work in the late 1930s, the St. Thomas Hospital in Akron was included.[13] Promoting their 4.25 by 4.25-inch bright enamel wall tiles, the

Tile height markers, Devola, Ohio lock.

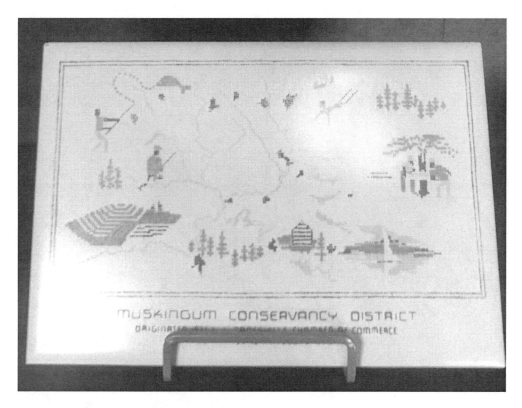

Tile replicating mural for Muskingum Watershed Conservancy District.

Mosaic Tile Company indicated that these floor and wall tiles were the "preferred materials in all modern hospital buildings due to their sanitary non-absorbent qualities and ability to resist wear and deterioration."[14] According to a news report, this hospital has claimed important "firsts" such as being the first "institutional home for Alcoholics Anonymous, operated the nation's first alcoholism treatment ward and was the first hospital in the nation to recognize alcoholism as a medical condition."[15] Now part of the larger system, Summa Health System, the building is still actively used.

California

"Eureka!" is what Archimedes reportedly shouted as he bathed and discovered displacement within water, and it is this legend that gold miners supposedly evoked when discovering gold in the 1840s in California.[16] Installed in the first floor of the California State Capitol building in 1896, a version of the State's seal was created by the Mosaic Tile Company.[17] This composite of tiles included the Roman goddess Minerva, symbolizing wisdom and war, and is the key focal point.[18] She is surrounded by a shield; a grizzly bear, symbolizing "strength and independence"; and shafts of grain, symbolizing the state's agriculture wealth.[19] Installed around the mosaic scene of the seal are background color tiles, border tiles of a circular pattern, and another border of a floral pattern. By 1982, a restoration effort was completed and brought in replicated tile designs to repair and replace the original Mosaic tile.[20]

Replicated tile of California State Capitol mural border.

Florida

A 100-foot mural on the exterior of a round building in Fort Lauderdale was designed with a sea horse, orange tree, gardenia bush, sailfish, blue heron, and trees and tropical plants.[21] Originally built with tile installed in 1964, the KenAnn building (sometimes spelled Kenann) was condemned due to severe safety issues in the 1990s.[22] The building had been vacant for years after the last owner declared bankruptcy. A new owner enlisted architect Dan Duckham in 1995 to restore the round building to its beauty while preserving the original mural tile.[23] The main building is eight stories tall with full glass windows. It is flanked by a square building with rounded angles on the part of the building which boasts the tile. Surrounded by palm trees and sparkling in the Florida sun, the building is incredibly unusual—modern and, at the same time, retro with the tiles.

Illinois

Renovated in 2014 into luxury apartments, what was originally the Lakeshore Athletic Club boasted that it was the training location for Olympic gold medalist and

Tarzan movie star Johnny Weissmuller.[24] Built in 1927 on Lakeshore Drive, Chicago, the indoor pool had a variety of Mosaic tile products installed which were described as "nautical-themed polychromatic enamel tiles found along the walls and floors surrounding the pool."[25] Described as 4-by-4 inch tiles with images of shells, crabs, seagulls, and fish, the "tiles were configured in 'sets' of seven tiles."[26] The tile was salvaged when the building underwent the 2014 renovation and the "original monogrammed stamp remains intact" on the back of the tiles to show the maker as Mosaic Tile Company.[27]

Listed on the National Register of Historic Places, the Union Park Hotel is an example of "apartment-hotels" specifically built after World War I for returning veterans and laborers in the near west side of Chicago.[28] As featured in the 1938 Mosaic Tile catalog, the company created the floor for the hotel lobby with three-quarter inch squares of unglazed tiles "arranged in a special modern design to harmonize with the interior architecture."[29] Within the 2010 application for National Registry status, the floors are described for this "modest means" hotel as "…large ceramic floor tiles in the main lobby that also feature Art Deco–style motifs."[30]

The 1938 catalog also provided a look at the use of faience tiles within the Disciples Divinity House Chapel at University of Chicago. The University described that the Chapel was part of a larger building for Divinity House which has 23 student rooms, a common room, a library, offices, and guest rooms along with the chapel.[31] This work was completed in 1928 in Collegiate Gothic style with arts and crafts influences. According to Mosaic Tile's catalog, the company worked on the faience floors leading to the front of the Chapel.[32]

Indiana

In 1938, the installation of tiles on the exterior of the Elwood, Indiana Coca-Cola Bottling Company was featured in a Mosaic Tile catalog of products. The photo in the brochure does not give a lot of detail as it is in black and white, but a local Elwood newspaper described the exterior changes with "an entirely new front … installed, tile being used to face the front of the building, and a large Coca-Cola sign being cut out of heavy aluminum."[33]

The Allen County Courthouse in Fort Wayne, built in 1902, underwent preservation work in the early 2000s after more than 100 years in service.[34] A guide written in 1913 described the interior with "handsome mosaic floors of encaustic tiles in vestibules, lobbies, rotunda, and Commissioners' Court Room" and under the rotunda's dome, "the floors of encaustic tiles laid in rich mosaic design" is featured.[35] Confirmed as Mosaic Tile by the Allen County Courthouse Preservation Trust, "The encaustic floor tiles were made in Zaneville, [*sic*] Ohio by the then new process for creating inlaid designs invented by Herman C. Mueller (1854–1941) and Karl Langenbeck."[36]

Michigan

The Henry Ford Hospital in Detroit was described in the Mosaic Tile Company's 50th Anniversary Program as the first large order of color wall tile. The building was completed in 1921 and included "85,000 square feet of wall tile and 60,000 pieces of trim

Disciples Divinity House tile display (courtesy Special Collections Research Center, University of Chicago Library).

Henry Ford Hospital, Detroit, Mich.

Henry Ford Hospital postcard, Detroit, Michigan.

tile."[37] Based on the industrial and automotive expansion in the United States, and notably in the Detroit area, Henry Ford recognized that for his growing workforce to meet the demands for autos, he wanted to keep "a healthy and productive community, and he envisioned creating a hospital for the working man."[38] Initially, the building was incomplete when it was given to the federal government in 1918 for use as a U.S. Army General Hospital to provide care for returning World War I veterans. The hospital was completed after the end of the war and opened in 1921 with 500 new beds for the growing Detroit area.[39] This hospital still serves the Detroit community as part of the Henry Ford Health System and strives to maintain its mission "to provide exceptional quality, cost effective care strengthened by education and research, carrying on the traditions of the founder and the original staff of the Henry Ford Hospital."[40]

Missouri

Two Mosaic Tile murals had been installed in Cape Girardeau in 1947 and featured images of the printing and newspaper industries. Both are located on the side of the *Southeast Missourian* newspaper building on Lorimer Street. According to newspaper historian Sharon K. Sanders, she found hand-written notes attributing the design of the murals to St. Louis muralist Ary Marbain, working with Mosaic Tile.[41] The design was transferred onto clay tiles by Mosaic Tile's artist, Ruth Axline, who also worked for other Muskingum County area potteries. The Mosaic Tile Company prepared the tiles for firing and sent those to Cape Girardeau for installation. Both murals are made of 6-inch tiles, and the final scenes 8 foot by 10 foot.

The first mural, "Art of Printing," features a collage of the printing processes and equipment, typesetting machines, presses, and finished products such as books and papers. The "Gathering & Disseminating News" mural, according to Sanders, focused on newsmakers who would be locally known leaders.[42] The mural itself depicts men and women engaged in various aspects of news making, discussing, writing, photography, traveling, and the printing of papers.

New York

New York's annual "Pace-Setter" house could be likened to today's example of the ultimate home that is highlighted on home improvement television shows. Mosaic Tile created a featured product as part of the Pace-Setter house; the company's homebuilding reputation paid off with national recognition. Mosaic's artistic designer Kenneth Gale spent two years working with the architects and staff of the *House Beautiful* magazine in constructing a model home, known as the Pace-Setter home, in Dobbs Ferry, New York.[43] The home was designed to include the latest in-home decorating features. The final cost of the home totaled $125,000 and included luxurious fabrics, furniture, appliances, and, of course, tiles (converted to 2020 value at $1.24 million).[44] The show house was open for public viewing during which do-it-yourself homeowners could order supplies that were featured in the home. The May 1951 issue of the magazine seemed to reflect the stereotypical thought of the day that a woman's place was in the home, since it was advertised as a house for "Future Living" and was "a one-woman, servantless, American-Style home."[45] Several local newspapers promoted opportunities for the Zanesville area community to listen to Gale's presentations about the home featuring the technology of the day: color slides.[46]

The Pace-Setter home in New York was not the first time Mosaic Tile was involved in such designing of model homes. A 1951 *Times Recorder* article boasted that the company had been involved in a "famous" Widdicomb Furniture Company home designed by the "famous" T.H. Robsjohn-Gibbings in 1950.[47] Another *House Beautiful* home one year earlier, in May 1950, also featured this furniture work by Robsjohn-Gibbings.[48] There was also a "holiday house" for *Holiday* magazine in 1950 featuring the tile in the interior and exterior of the home.[49] The article indicated that the "new Mosaic tile is so economical in the long run that it fits in the most moderate budget for home building."[50] Apparently, radiant heating was the new way for homebuilders to warm homes, and a study by the American Institute for Architects, cited in a 1951 *Times Recorder* article, confirmed the "adaptability of tile in this heating medium."[51]

Less specific information is available for Mosaic Tile's involvement in the tiling of the Holland Tunnel for automobile transport under the Hudson River. Several resources, including the company's 50th Anniversary Program, indicated that Mosaic's tile was used in the tunnel along with Zanesville's other important tile factory, American Encaustic Tiling Company.[52] When opened in 1927, the Port Authority of New York and New Jersey reported that over 2.9 million wall tiles and 3.1 million ceiling tiles were installed, but details of the types of tiles are not provided—just the generic, lower case "mosaic tile" usually describes the tile.[53] Located somewhere in the middle of the tunnel, symbolically thought to be where New York and New Jersey meet, is a vertical display of red and blue tiles with horizontal tiles making rectangular shapes surrounding the states' names in lighter blue, yellow, and red tiles. Otherwise, the walls are lined with mostly white square tiles throughout.

House Beautiful magazine transferred image on tote.

Holland Tunnel, New York City, New York (courtesy Dr. Rebecca Watts).

Pennsylvania

Originally built as the Pendleton House and renamed in 1946, the Colonel Drake Hotel was a wood frame construction in 1864 when it began its more than 100-year history serving the visitors of Titusville.[54] The building was renovated in 1897, and Mosaic Tile was used for patterned floor tiles.[55] The Company advertised this connection when the Zanesville area was opening a J.C. Penney in 1960 when Mosaic Tile announced that one of the company's "earliest installations was the Colonel Drake Hotel" (at the time of the installation in the late 1890s, the hotel was called the Mansion House).[56] When renovated in 1947, the new owner found that the tile floor had been covered with a "succession of carpets and linoleums."[57] Though it is hard to see details, the floor tiles appeared to be a large floral design. In 1960, Mosaic claimed that the "tiled lobby floor there showed no wear after 64 years, when the hotel was recently renovated"[58]; however, the new owner indicated that "the tile can't be effectively restored, so it will again be covered."[59] Unfortunately, the building was torn down in the early 2000s and replaced with a building housing a pharmacy.[60]

Tennessee

Promoted within the Mosaic Tile Company's 1938 catalog, the Coca-Cola Bottling Plant in Memphis had a black and white photo of the new plant's factory floor.[61] Mosaic indicated that "Flint Tile was selected after tests were made of other flooring materials."[62] It is unfortunate that no color photos have been found of this floor and the ledge of the machinery's curb, as the floor is described as "a checkerboard design composed of 6 × 6 units of Green and White Flint tile, while the curb is of special glazed plastic faience. The large faience tile Coca-Cola plaques are in the natural colors and provide an interesting feature."[63]

Texas

The 1936 construction of the Will Rogers Coliseum and Auditorium in Fort Worth, Texas, included two Mosaic Tile friezes which were each 10 feet tall by 200 feet long.[64] Using mostly 9 inch by 9 inch tiles with a "special faience body," the mural is made of two composites.[65] Kenneth Gale is credited with these designs, and the Zanesville newspaper proclaimed that Gale was "well known in national artistic circles, his most famous work probably being the design for the Dallas, Texas, memorial."[66] (Fort Worth is about 30 miles west of Dallas.) The facility was built in commemoration of the Texas centennial and served as a public entertainment, sports, and livestock complex.[67] Fortunately, these special murals are still in existence and share "the settlement and industrial development of the West, while the coliseum depicted the various settlers who shaped the cultural heritage of the Southwest."[68] In 2020, community concern was raised about the depiction of Black males who appear to be picking cotton. Some community members interpreted the scene as one showing the men as slaves while an opposing interpretation indicated that, because the men were wearing coveralls, the men were sharecroppers and not slaves.[69] The city conducted public hearings and after great input decided to leave the mural in its original state but add historical context for visitors to read and better understand the 1936 design.

Washington, D.C.

Now called the National Building Museum (formerly the Pension Building), this federal building had the Great Seal of the United States tile composite installed in the courtyard to commemorate the second inauguration of President William McKinley in 1901.[70] Described as a "heavy Damask design, resembling fabric, that was used to decorate the tiles," this Seal matches the tile display on the lockmaster's house built in Marietta in 1899.[71] At the time, the D.C. building housed the Pension Building but was vacated in 1926 to house several other federal agencies until the 1960s.[72] The D.C. building was not in good condition, and it was not used for nearly 20 years when in 1978 the building was preserved "as a national treasure" following a Congressional resolution.[73] Renamed, "the National Building Museum opened in 1985" and continues to operate.[74]

Though a set of 19 tiles may not have been initially meant for the White House library's fireplace, that is where Mosaic Tile Company's product was installed. Designed by Mosaic's Artistic Director, Kenneth Gale, in 1945, President Franklin Roosevelt planned the symbols and designs of the tiles that he wanted to commemorate for the fireplace surround.[75] He and his daughter Anna wanted to portray buildings and majestic images in Washington, D.C., such as the U.S. Capitol, the Jefferson Memorial, the White House, and several others. Edwin Morris, assistant supervisor of the U.S. Public Buildings Administration, reported that Roosevelt was planning for these tiles to be installed

White House fireplace tile featuring the White House (courtesy Ohio History Connection (H66747) at the National Road & Zane Grey Museum).

White House fireplace tile featuring the Seal of the President of the United States (courtesy Ohio History Connection (H66744) at the National Road & Zane Grey Museum).

at his home, Hyde Park; however, the tiles were ultimately installed in the White House library.[76] The White House tiles stayed in place until the 1962 Kennedy-era redesign.[77]

West Virginia

The city of Weirton's founder, Ernest T. Weir, provided a financial gift from his charitable foundation to break ground for a new public library in 1956.[78] Named in honor of his wife, the Mary H. Weir Public Library was opened in 1958, one year after Ernest Weir died. Designed by Byron Shrider, the library's mural in the children's activity room measured 10 feet by 54 feet and was made of "1 1/16-inch squares of unglazed Granitex mosaics with glazed embellishments."[79] The mural design was of Western culture, "namely the Hebrew, Greek, and Roman civilizations and the arts and sciences of their time."[80]

Panama Canal

An amazing feat affecting the entire world was the construction and opening of the Panama Canal in 1914.[81] The United States bought out the French interest for $40 million in 1902 after that country's failed attempt to connect the 50 miles between the Atlantic and Pacific Oceans. This project was monumental and dangerous with over 5,600 individuals killed during nearly 10 years of work.[82] Only one source can be found connecting the Mosaic Tile Company to the Canal, and very few know of this information.[83] In addition to installing tile for floors, walls, and restrooms, Mosaic created "gauges for registering the depth of the water in the locks of the canal."[84] These gauges needed to be made of "material that would be as lasting as the locks themselves."[85] Mosaic's gauges were put

Panama Canal postcard.

into use at three locks along the canal leading up to the 1914 opening. Additionally, "vitrified floor and glazed tiling used in the Gatun hydroelectric station; the Gatun, Miraflores, and Pedro Miguel control house, and the tiling for the baths and lavatories of the Tivoli hotel."[86] The final location of Mosaic tile for the canal was on the floors and walls of the administration building. With the expansion work that began in 2006, it is difficult to ascertain if any of the original Mosaic Tile products are still in use.[87]

S.S. America

Not being limited to land based architecture, the Mosaic Tile Company contributed to the swimming pool and kitchen of the luxury liner, the S.S. *America*.[88] Intended to be a grand cruise ship, the *America* was considered a "perfect ship."[89] The three sidewalls of the natatorium were covered with light to dark blue tiles.[90] On the fourth wall, a silver tile was installed and, although it was never used for this purpose before, special research was conducted by Mosaic Tile's engineers to use the silver tiles as markers with the depths of the pool identified along the sides.[91] On the deck of the pool, an unglazed treated tile was used so that the floor would not be slippery. In the kitchen, high glaze tiles were used which "will not permit absorption of moisture or grease."[92] Due to the start of World War II, the S.S. *America* was quickly converted to serve the United States Navy in 1941 to transport over 8,000 service men and women into service and was renamed the USS *West Point*.[93] After World War II and many years of switching from owner to owner and being renamed multiple times, the ship was headed for the scrap pile until it was purchased for possible refurbishing to be a cruise ship again. While being towed to its destination, the ship encountered a huge storm and was stranded at the Canary Islands.[94] Over time the vessel rusted, and it sank into the sea in 2009.[95]

S.S. Zanesville *Victory*

While not a permanently installed floor or wall feature, Mosaic Tile created a plaque to be displayed on the S.S. *Zanesville* Victory Ship.[96] The plaque, designed by Ruth Axline, featured a Y-Bridge image and was titled "Y Bridge from Putnam Hill."[97] The ship launched in 1945 for service in World War II and later in the Korean and Vietnam wars. The S.S. *Zanesville* was "mothballed" in 1946 and then later scrapped.[98]

These examples of Mosaic Tile Company work within Ohio, in other states, and around the world are extensive; however, there are likely many more that were not documented. In an effort to preserve a historical record of sources and installation sites, the Appendix provides a compilation of several newspaper articles, catalogs, or other sources which mentioned the sites; however, very little information was found, and these sites were not reviewed in this chapter.

As time slips by and memories fade, we may not ever know the full reach that the Mosaic Tile Company had around the world during its years of operation. Regardless, the ingenuity and creativity from Zanesville, Ohio, can be seen in surprising places—we all need to take a critical look at the tiles that surround us.

10

Animals and Paperweights
and Trivets, Oh My!

The Mosaic Tile Company's primary product of floor and wall tiles were functional, yet the artistic scenes that the company created allowed for creativity in homes and large buildings nationwide. Over the years, the company also created giftware or promotional items, which have become highly collectible. When the Depression slowed business, the company began making hot plates, badges, boxes, bookends, souvenirs, and wall panels to generate revenue.[1] Other pieces included a cookie jar; paperweights; coasters; ashtrays; dog, bear, turtle, and bison figurines; and Jasperware-style memorial paperweights. Made in limited quantities or for only special occasions, the rarity of these items causes the re-sale value to climb in auctions and online bidding sites. Since the company was primarily known for functional tiles, the artistry of the limited giftware items seemed to be overlooked at the time of production. Today, online auction sites demand high dollars for some Mosaic Tile Company pieces. Though exact dates when pieces were produced are generally unknown, most are considered to have been made after World War II; however, a few do have dates imprinted that might indicate when these were produced.

Key to confirming that the Mosaic Tile Company was the producer of these pieces is the mark that can often be found on the reverse or bottom of the item. Over the years, the company primarily used two marks. Occasionally, the company used some variation on printed pieces such as stylized on their catalogs, but two primary marks are best identified with the company. The first was an intertwined "MTC" within a circle. This seemed to be the original mark in the late 1890s and was used through the early 1900s. At some point in the first 20 to 30 years of the 1900s, a racetrack oval shape with MOSAIC in all capital letters was added as the company's primary mark and was used most often through the final years of the company's production. Sigafoose determined that this new mark was introduced in the 1920s.[2] Lage's source of marks indicated that this second mark was used between 1930 and 1964.[3] Additional authoritative books described the marks: Barber's 1909 edition and Thorn's 1947 book shows only the intertwined initials within a circle; the book by Wires, Schneider, and Mesre from 1972 shows three marks—the two mentioned previously and then the negative image of the racetrack oval; and Lehner's from 1978 describes the two primary marks.[4] Within the Zanesville City Directory, the company paid for advertisements in nearly every publication. The intertwined letters and circle mark was used within the ad until the 1939–1940 publication when the racetrack oval was used.[5] Even the white and brick four-story building on the Mosaic Tile property, built in the early 1900s, featured the intertwined initials.

Mosaic Tile Company intertwined letters in circle mark.

Mosaic Tile Company racetrack oval mark.

(Left to right) Zane's Trace Commemoration 6 × 6 inch tile dated 1974; U.S. Bicentennial 4 × 4 inch tile dated 1776–1976; "Only 'Y' Bridge in the U.S." 4 × 4 inch tile; "Member of Zanesville Muskingum County Chamber of Commerce" 6 × 6 inch tile reproduced to replicate a 1943 membership plaque, circa 2000.

Of course, collectors always need to be on the lookout for reproduction pieces. There are probably some pieces that were made purposely to fool collectors while other items, such as plain tiles, may have been painted or decorated at home. Another popular and difficult to find item, a cookie jar, was also similarly made by other pottery companies. Reproductions are often found instead. It takes practice and time to spot fakes, to appreciate creativity, and to be wary of spending money on the reproductions.

The Practical and the Creative

Kitchen and Bath Items

Several examples of the practical and creative have been found in a residential home just northwest of the Zanesville downtown area built in 1930. This home's kitchen and bathrooms are complete with tiles on floors and walls. The color scheme of the kitchen tile is blue in varying shades. One nook of the room has a built-in arched cupboard mimicking the arched ceiling; the entire area was covered with square and rectangular blue tiles.

Within one bathroom of that home, the tile colors are variations of light to dark tan. Accent color tiles at the mid-level of the wall and around the perimeter of the floor are in dark blue rectangular tiles. Other tiles in the room are white. In addition to the plain wall and floor tiles are molded tiles in the shape of towel hooks, toilet paper roll holders, and dish soap holders.

Above the tub within the tiled shower surround of this first bathroom is an archway of the tan and dark blue tiles. The feature of the shower is a panel, or composite, of several tiles that together create the image of two peacocks facing each other on branches

Kitchen with blue tiles in north Zanesville home (courtesy Jerri L. Elson).

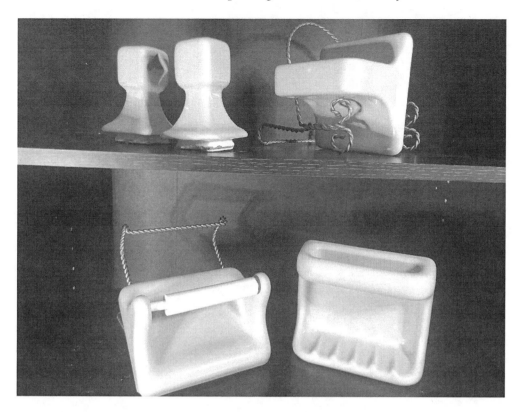

Sample household functional items for kitchen or bath.

with the sun in the background. This composite is made up of three vertical tiles and five horizontal tiles. The colors of this mural are bright solid colors with a blue sky and green leaves holding the two peacocks in the middle. The wings of the birds are primarily a bold black with spots of aqua and red throughout. The birds' bodies are a deep dark blue and their faces are brown with black and mauve features. A remarkably similar scene was depicted in the Purviances' book of art tile as "a watercolor design signed by Karl Bergman."[6] Bergman, according to this book, had originally worked for a year at Mosaic Tile but was lured away by an American Encaustic Tiling Company's executive for more money.

A second full bathroom at this home is primarily made up of pink and white tiles. Again, the archway over the tub calls attention to the primary pink square tiles with accent rectangular green tiles. The featured composite is of a sailboat. Made up of five vertical square tiles and seven horizontal square tiles, coming together to create the artwork, the sailboat looks like a watercolor painting with shades of blues, greens, mauves, yellows, and outlined with black lines. The sailboat is on a calm sea with various vibrant blue and green colors. Another sailboat is in the distant and seagulls are flying near the first boat. A similar scene is part of the 1939 company catalog.[7]

These homes mirrored my own childhood home. Thanks to the Kauffmann family (see Preface), the kitchen, hallway, basement, and breezeway were decorated with various shapes, sizes, and colors of tiles. For example, one hallway's ceiling was arched with blue tiles spanning the floors and over the entire ceiling. Intermixed with plain tiles were utilitarian pieces made of the tile such as outlet covers and light switches. Other examples

Shower surround with peacock feature in north Zanesville home (courtesy Jerri L. Elson).

Shower surround with sailboat feature in north Zanesville home (courtesy Jerri L. Elson).

Outlet covers.

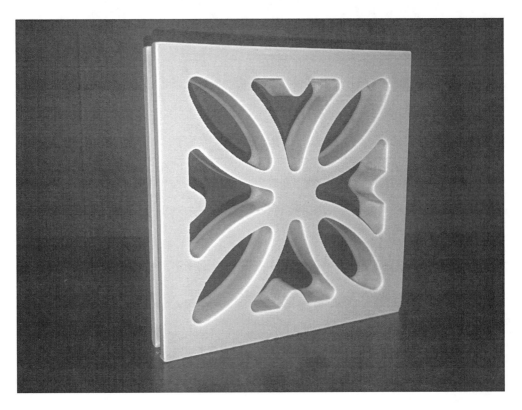

Furnace vent cover.

Exterior staircase and sidewalk.

Exterior basement wall.

have been found of utilitarian items such as furnace face covers, vent covers, hooks, and various others.

As shown in samples of entryways and building exteriors, the tiles at my family's home also were installed on an exterior staircase and basement wall. A combination of two colors and styles, the rise of each stair was comprised of six tan tiles (six-inch by six-inch) and the run was made of two rows of six reddish-brown tiles that had the appearance of four smaller tiles on each. The exterior wall of the basement also had six-inch by six-inch tan plain tiles.

Decorative Tiles

Mosaic produced a line of decorative tiles for use surrounding fireplaces or to use as accents within wainscoting or other installments on walls and floors. The catalog of 1939 featured fireplace faience mantels and faience inserts and strips.[8] Similarly, in the 1949 Company catalog, the decorative tiles were shown and described as "popular for many purposes—fireplaces, window sills, hot plates for table settings, wall plaques, table tops, etc."[9] Various styles could be selected if ordering from the company. In general, plain tiles would be used as the background on the left and right and across the top of the fireplace opening. Throughout those three areas, accent tiles with various scenes or flowers or other images would be inserted. Several types of decorative tiles were produced for a wide variety of choices. Eventually, these tiles were not only used on fireplaces, but anywhere accents or decorative tile might be needed. These are tiles that can often be found in antique stores in 4-inch and 6-inch or other sizes in rectangular shape while this book has many samples, there are many more not depicted.

Not specifically found in a catalog, there seemed to be an effort to create various

Decorative tile samples.

"series" of decorative tiles with varied themes such as the Patriot series, with "minutemen" portrayed; automobiles, primarily very early versions of cars; animals and birds; churches and other significant buildings; people dressed in Amish-wear; fruits; geometric shapes, florals, and ships. Other series included what has been termed a "Kindergarten" series of cartoonish figures and the twelve zodiac figures.

Significant images portrayed two literary series: William Crane's illustrations of *Aesop's Fables* and Omar Khayyam's *Rubaiyat*. William Crane illustrated many of *Aesop's Fables* and these illustrations have been transferred onto several tiles. One source indicated that these tiles were produced with an identical process which included creating the design on a sheet of tissue paper that was transferred onto the tile.[10] The tissue could be used by that original company or could be purchased, "resulting in the same motif being produced by more than one tile maker."[11] According to Edward Fitzgerald's version of the transcribed *Rubaiyat*, this was a "collection of mystical verses" by Khayyam who was an 11th-century "poet, astronomer, and mathematician."[12] Fitzgerald indicated that Khayyam's work is a "rumination on the nature of fate, death, love, and the transience of life," which ended up labeling Khayyam as a rebel in those years. Mosaic Tile reproduced a few of these images on tiles for decorative displays. A few companies, including American Encaustic Tiling and Mosaic Tile, reproduced these images in similar fashion.

Though there always seems to be one more decorative tile that needs to be added to this author's collection, there is a method to the madness. In order to document as many tiles created by the Mosaic Tile Company photographs as possible, many are included in the color inserts.

Hot Plates or Trivets

In a 1958 Company newsletter, *The Mosaic Times,* hot plates were introduced as "a service to employees."[13] These 15 different hot plates in the newsletter were available for purchase by employees for "67.5 cents each." All were 6 by 6 inches and could be used as "hot plates or wall plaques."[14] Also sometimes referred to as trivets, many are available at antique stores and are obviously to be used to hold hot items given the four felt

Hot plates/trivets samples.

feet often found on the reverse along with a hook for wall hanging. Some, unfortunately, are not easy to identify as Mosaic, as the logo is raised but very faint on many of the tiles.

Functional Kitchen Items

Generally seen as items needed for the kitchen, a pitcher, small bowls, a tray, and a vase have been identified as Mosaic Tile products with recognizable trademarks. A green pitcher, conserved by Muskingum County History, is without decoration; it is a simple pitcher approximately 10 inches tall with a rounded handle and a spout on the rim. Another functional piece is a small yellow round bowl. This light-yellow bowl is approximately 1.75-inches tall and 4.75 inches in diameter. This bowl has the intertwined logo on the bottom along with both the Zanesville and New York locations, dating this piece at the earliest to 1901. A small pink bowl, 2.5 inches in diameter across the opening, 1.75 inches at the base, and 1.5 inches tall, has the racetrack mark on the bottom. A large green tray has been featured for sale on an online auction site as well as within Lage's marks book identifying the product as Mosaic Tile Company. The online site indicated that the tray is turquoise green and is 7 inches in width, 11.25 inches in length, and 1.625 inch in height.[15] Very few details are available about a green vase that had been featured in the Purviances' book focused on Zanesville Art Tile. It is photographed and appears to be a very dark green color. The description is "6-inch vase with pinecone decoration."[16]

Saucers

The purpose or function of small diamond-shaped saucers or trays with the profile of a horse's head is unknown at this point and no resources were found that describe these. The saucers were flat with a raised horsehead in the middle and seem to be functional for butter pats or some other dinner item or perhaps a small ashtray. The saucer has an edge or lip around the diamond shape and is about 5.5 inches left to right and 3.25 inches on the shorter top to bottom. Usually found in pastel shades of blue, yellow, green, and pink, this set of small saucers does not usually have the Mosaic Tile logo on it.

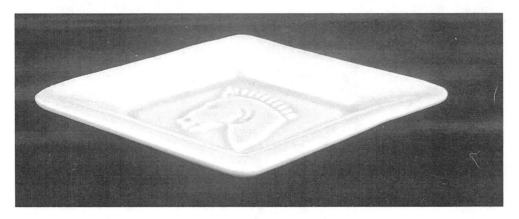

Horse's head saucer.

Coasters

A few different sizes and styles of round coasters in light pastel colors with various flowers as the primary feature were created by the company. The larger coaster is 3.5 inches in diameter while the smaller flower coaster is 3 inches. This style of coaster has a glazed finish with the base of the coaster a slightly darker hue of the color. These coasters do not usually have the mark of the company on the bottom but can sometimes be seen along the narrow rim with "Made in USA." An online auction site listed a box set of 8 coasters and included a photo of the label within the box. The label indicated that the coasters were "Courtesy of the Zanesville Banks: The First National Bank, the Citizens National Bank and the First Trust & Savings Bank."[17] The auction described the boxed set as a "Zanesville Banks Premium" and that the coasters were "used as a premium for customers" of the banks.[18] Another type of round floral coaster is 3.5 inches in diameter, but these coasters are an ivory color overall with raised and painted leaves and flowers in purple, green, orange, yellow, blue, peach, and perhaps other colors. These coasters often have the name of Mosaic in all capital letters next to Made in USA around the narrow rim of the tile.

Another set of four round coasters features a single swan on each one. These coasters feature swans that are bright white on backgrounds of deep green, black, red, and blue. The coaster's edge is also white matching the swan. These coasters are also different on the base. Covered completely with a cork substance, the oval racetrack mark is printed in ink on the cork and the words "Swan White" are printed in script lettering. This connects to the 1939 catalog of the company which boasts that Mosaic had created a new white color for tile making.[19] The catalog announced that since many shades of white are in the "off-white range," the Mosaic Tile Company had created "in Swan White a new, improved, highly craze-resistant glaze vastly superior in purity and opacity to the regular

Floral coasters (single colors).

white glaze wall tile."[20] The catalog indicated that customers "could request samples of this Swan White creation …."[21] Perhaps these coasters were given to potential clients to promote the new glaze.

Ashtrays

Today, ashtrays have "all but disappeared as a visible accessory of modern life."[22] In the days of Mosaic Tile's operation, ashtrays were standard décor in many homes. Many of Mosaic Tile's decorative designs of ashtrays reflected very funky geometric patterns from the 1950s. An unusual ashtray was created in what is sometimes described as an "atomic" shape. This type of ashtray can usually be found in green or turquoise color. This freeform shape is likely from the late 1950s when this design was introduced in the space age Sputnik era.[23] The photographed ashtray is 7 inches across on the largest width area and narrows to about 2.5 inches toward the pointed front. The ashtray stands about 8 inches tall.

Dog ashtray (courtesy Jeffrey Snyder).

Another type of ashtray was angular, five-sided with a deep center and various rounded spaces for cigarettes presumably to be placed. This ashtray had a dog resting atop one side and even the dog had an angular shape rather than rounded. This ashtray has been seen in a greenish turquoise, brown, and likely other colors. Similar pieces have been found on auction sites with the Mosaic racetrack oval.

Another example was a hexagonal shaped ashtray with rounded sides. There is a rounded space in the front for cigarettes to be placed and one of the sides is extended upward, higher than the others, similar to a smokestack chimney, perhaps designed to hold a small box of matches. This ashtray also came in multiple colors and is 4.25 inches across and 4 inches from back to front. It is 2.5 inches tall.

Finally, the "practical" need for an ashtray and advertisement of the company came together with a racetrack oval shape with the capital MOSAIC name in the middle. This ashtray has been seen in antique stores in typically a green color and is approximately 7 inches long and 3 inches wide.

An unusually shaped white ashtray was spotted online (and likely others will surface in the future).[24] This piece seems to be a merging of two shapes. The front is a square shape, and the back is a rounded cup-like shape with a flat bottom. On the front, the company name is arched over the opening where the square and the cup meet. At the bottom of the front facing is "Zanesville OH" and "New York NY."

A small ashtray, perhaps used by a single person during a game of cards, was an oval shaped white base and bordered with prime color flower shapes in bright blue, yellow, red, and green leaves. The oval shape is 3" × 4.75" and there is a small dip on one end of the oval, presumably to rest a cigarette.

Medallions

The earliest souvenirs for which records can be noted are commemorative medallions in honor of an event or person. One such event was to honor the Cyrene commandery number 10 of the Knights Templar of the Grand Lodge of Knights of Pythias from 1899.[25] These honorary souvenirs were tiles created to look like military style medals or badges. The newspaper article indicated that 8,000 badges were "small tile souvenirs" that would have been distributed to the "Knights who will gather" at the event that was held in Cincinnati.[26] The badge is hexagonal and attached to a ribbon and metal ring and pin for a lapel. This medallion measures 2.25 inches from top to bottom with "raised relief designs."[27]

Another round medallion was made for the Rotary Club of Zanesville. No details can be found to tell of the year or reason this was produced. This item was found in Sigafoose's book described as a "disc ... meant to be worn around the neck, hanging on a string or ribbon."[28] The medallion measures 2.375 inches in diameter. The reverse side bears the intertwined MTC mark along with the company name and Zanesville, Ohio.

These medallions are a rare find in today's antique markets, but one example of this round medallion that survived for more than 100 years is from the dedication of the new Bethesda Hospital on August 20, 1916. In addition to the event information, an image of two staffs, a sword, and three linked oval rings are intertwined. The staffs, sword, and three linked rings can be found as part of the symbol for the Grand Lodge of Ohio and

Knights of Pythias medallion (courtesy David M. Taylor).

the Independent Order of Odd Fellows.[29] According to Schneider's book about Bethesda Hospital, the "Ohio Grand Lodge of Masons laid the cornerstone of the new building" and the Lodge "dedicated the new structure" during the opening ceremonies on August 20.[30] The medallion is approximately 2.5 inches in diameter and has the company name and the intertwined logo on the reverse.

While not marked with a date, another medallion is hexagonal and features an elk's head with antlers and the phrases "No. 114" and "Zanesville, O.," this piece may be tied to the Elk Lodge, number 114, that was previously active in Zanesville. The organization built a new facility on Fourth Street in downtown Zanesville in 1912 and perhaps this item was used as a souvenir.[31]

Rotary Club of Zanesville medallion.

Bethesda Hospital medallion.

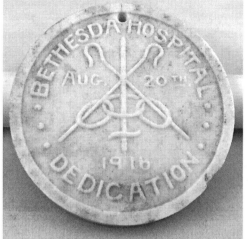

Zanesville Elk's medallion (courtesy David M. Taylor).

Jasperware-style Paperweights

The Mosaic Tile Company must have been called on by many companies and organizations to create souvenir paperweights for special events. Sometimes these items
were made exclusively for an event, while others, such as the Abraham Lincoln hexagonal paperweight to be described, was reproduced for several special occasions or advertisements. According to one source, these paperweights were created around the time of
World War I.[32] As seen in the photograph of the author's collection, most of these individuals are historical figures and will be described further.

The original Jasperware was invented in 1774 by English pottery maker Josiah
Wedgwood. This line of pottery is best known for its light "Wedgwood blue" color
with a "smooth texture, lovely matte finish."[33] No specific inventory of the number of
Jasperware-style Mosaic Tile paperweights has been found nor a timeline showing when
these were made, or for which event these were produced. Interestingly, there seems to
have been several companies that created similar paperweights, and according to an article in *Flash Point*, the hexagonal molds were used by many companies including Mosaic
and Cambridge Tile Company.[34] How more than one company obtained the mold or
which was the first to use is unclear.

The Abraham Lincoln paperweight had been produced for several purposes, and this
is one of those images that seems to have been produced using the same or similar mold
by more than just Mosaic Tile. One source indicated that the hexagonal paperweight was
first produced in 1909 in honor of the 16th American president's 100th anniversary of his
birth; his "Centenary."[35] The Lincoln paperweight was also created in honor of, or perhaps for the fundraising efforts of, the re-election campaign for Illinois Senator Everett
Dirksen in either 1962 or 1968 since the back of the tile is marked with "Senator Everett M. Dirksen" in all capital letters.[36] Of course, the Mosaic Tile Company in Zanesville
closed in 1967, so it is unclear for which year these were produced or if another company
had produced those later tiles. Another online source indicated that the cameo paperweights were "copied by the Cambridge Art Tile Works … of Covington, Kentucky."[37] The
source speculated that it was "possible that Cambridge bought or leased the Lincoln tile
mold from Mosaic."[38] There are several examples on the market of this item also used for
advertising for a specific company such as for the Allen Tiling Company with that name
featured on the back of the tile. Usually this paperweight, approximately 3 inches by 3.5
inches, was made in the Wedgwood blue, but has been seen in other colors in addition to
a cast iron metal.

Other popular, and harder to find, hexagonal paperweights include Woodrow Wilson, Benjamin Franklin, Christopher Columbus, Robert Treat, José Martí, Simón Bolívar, David Lloyd George, and, a cartoonish figure, a billiken. (Even harder to find are the
cardboard boxes in which these were originally packaged.) Since the company did not
distribute an inventory list, there can be confusion on some of the images. The men on
the paperweights are in cameo or profile pose. Most readers will easily know the profiles
of Lincoln, America's 16th president; Wilson, the 28th president; Franklin, a U.S. Founding Father and prolific inventor; and Columbus, the Italian explorer credited with discov-
ery of the Americas. However, all the other featured men may not be as well known.

Styled with a "Pilgrim" hat (and so the tile is often named "Pilgrim"), Robert Treat
entered into an "agreement to take up lots on the Passaic River … which they named
New Ark or Newark," thus founding Newark, New Jersey, in 1666.[39] Treat was chosen as

Deputy Governor and later Governor of Connecticut from 1682 to 1698.[40] The paperweight shown in the photograph has on the reverse that the tile was created for the 250th anniversary celebration of Newark, New Jersey, in 1916.

José Martí was a poet and journalist who fought for Cuban independence from Spain in the late 1890s.[41] This tile has on the reverse "Sucursal-Galaiano" which was the name of a bank in Havana. No date is given on this tile.

Not found in any pottery or ceramic art resources, the Simón Bolívar hexagonal tile includes a man in military uniform facing left. Bolívar was a military leader for Venezuela involved in the revolutions for independence from Spain in 1810.[42] The Republic of Bolivia "was created in honor of the inspirational leader."[43] The reverse side of the tile has several abbreviations, but notably "Buenos Aires," "Gratry," and "Rosario" are prominent words. Rosario is one of the largest Argentinian cities and is northwest of Buenos Aires, which is the largest city.[44]

Another mystery figure on a Jasperware-style paperweight is possibly David Lloyd George, Prime Minister of the United Kingdom from 1916 to 1922. When comparing publicly available images of Lloyd George to the tile image, there do seem to be some similarities, but this may never be fully confirmed.[45] The only other possible link to confirm the connection is on the reverse of the tile with the initials, IM&TD. The IM&TD was the Interstate Mantel and Tile Dealer association which held its annual conference in Buffalo in 1916, the same year Lloyd George became Prime Minister.[46] Another source indicated that this tile was the image of Thomas Marshall who was Woodrow Wilson's vice president.[47] A review of Buffalo, New York, newspapers for information about the conference and any possible connections did not make the link between Buffalo, IM&TD, Lloyd George or Marshall.

Have you heard of a billiken? Other than being an unusual college mascot for Saint Louis University, a billiken is a "mythical good-luck figure who represents 'things as they ought to be.'"[48] This figure can be found on various items, all intended to be fun, cute, and a source of good luck if you rub its stomach. The Mosaic Tile Company's billiken holds its clues on the front of the tile, where the billiken is facing forward with a sash across its chest with "Pittsburgh Court" and its feet are marked with "No 2 R J." Muskingum County History provided the information that the paperweight was made for the Pittsburgh Court of the Royal Order of Jesters.[49] The Pittsburgh Court was founded in 1941 and adopted its icon of the billiken image.[50]

Another non-human Jasperware-style paperweight is of the New York Rotary International. The Jasperware blue hexagonal base has the white shield attached in the middle with a large capital "NY" for New York above the Rotary club's shield emblem. The emblem has the standard Rotary wheel with "Rotary International" around the wheel. The hexagonal tile is 3 inches by 3.5 inches with the company trademark on the back.[51]

Marked on the front of this hexagonal tile is March 14, 1911, for the Grand Council meeting of the Ohio Electric Railway Beneficial Association (OERBA). According to a newspaper advertisement in 1911, the Ohio Electric Railway had travel options from Zanesville to Muncie and Middleton to Buckeye Lake. The OERBA was described as an organization "conducted by the company's employees."[52] The association received donations from the Ohio Electric Railway and "employee initiation fees, dues, and death assessments" and supported "operating expenses, sick benefits, and death claims."[53] The event commemorated on the hexagonal tile seems to have been tied to the annual meeting of the Grand Council, which was held on March 17; however, there was no explanation evident for the date of March 11 in Zanesville.[54]

Like the hexagonal paperweights, Mosaic did a few oval-shaped Jasperware tiles in the same way. One that can be found more often than others is the General John J. "Black Jack" Pershing paperweight. Measuring larger than the hexagonal tiles, Pershing's oval tile is approximately 3.5 inches by 5.25 inches. President Wilson assigned Pershing to lead the American Expeditionary Force (AEF) in Europe during World War I. His leadership in integrating the AEF with the Allies led to the armistice with Germany in 1918.[55] The back of this tile is marked with "Zanesville Post No. 29 American Legion, Home Building Fund." In 1929, this American Legion teamed up with Mosaic Tile to produce 1,000 tiles that the Legion would sell for $1 each in order to support the funds needed to build a new "home" for the Legion gatherings.[56] These were sold at the state and national Legion conventions that year. A newspaper article also mentioned that the Pershing plaque would be the first to be created and sold, then Charles Lindbergh and President Woodrow Wilson tiles were planned next.[57] As mentioned earlier, the Wilson tile was hexagonal. A review of Lindbergh profile photos does not seem to match any of the documented tiles as of yet.

The George Washington paperweight in Mosaic Tile oval Jasperware measures 3 by 3.75 inches. Washington is facing right, and the reverse of the tile is plain with only the oval racetrack mark, unlike many others with various promotional messages or events.

Another oval Jasperware tile, possibly of Winston Churchill, was found on an online source.[58] Suspected to be Churchill, the source indicated that the image of the man is an "unidentified" figure on a large oval measuring 4.75 inches by 6.75 inches. According to the source, the reverse of the tile indicated "Made from all American material in America by Americans, Zanesville Tile Company, Zanesville, Ohio."[59] The actual Zanesville Tile Company was in operation from 1905 to 1909 as a sort of subsidiary of the J.B. Owens Pottery Company in Zanesville.[60] Churchill would have been serving in the British Parliament during those years after he had a successful military career in the late 1890s. It is doubtful that the Zanesville Tile Company produced this tile, but the reverse text would also have been unusual for the Mosaic Tile Company to have used. Sigafoose had an example of this oval paperweight attributed to Mosaic Tile Company; however, he did not identify the man as Churchill. He did note that on the reverse side, the name of Mosaic Tile Company was handwritten and not imprinted as with most of the tiles.[61]

Round Paperweights

A different type of paperweight that Mosaic created was round and typically 3 inches in diameter and much thicker than the other types of paperweights, at approximately 0.5 inch in depth. The reverse side of these paperweights was plain and usually had the racetrack oval MOSAIC mark impressed into the bottom surface (sometimes this mark was either omitted or covered by rough surface or cardboard-like finish). These, too, were usually produced in honor of an event or person, and were specifically made for souvenir or advertising purposes. Examples include events-focused Sesquicentennial of Zanesville in 1947; Bethesda Hospital opening in 1965; and Good Samaritan remodeling in 1966; advertising-focused for the Mosaic Tile Company in general and for its products; community-focused Rotary International and William M. Shinnick; and many others.

At least one round paperweight was created in honor of a person, William Shinnick, one of the founders and leaders of Mosaic Tile. Another round tile was an advertisement for Mosaic Tile Company itself with the name "W.V. Stafford" in the center. Stafford was an eastern United States representative for the company based in New York City.[62] Perhaps Mr. Stafford would hand these to prospective customers. Another tile seemed to be something for anyone on the sales team to provide to customers as it listed all the different types of tiles such as faience, Granitex, Harmonitone, and others that were often seen listed in sales catalog. Other examples include promoting the Zanesville Rotary Club, West Point, and other businesses, as well as some round paperweights with simple geometric shapes and plain colors.

Animals

Mosaic designers seemed to favor many animals, exotic and domesticated. One of the first designs sometime in the early 1900s was a tile with an elephant balancing on a ball. This seemed to be a popular pose and was either copied by other companies or Mosaic designers copied it themselves.[63] The seller of a tile with this image on an online auction site indicated that his tile was "probably a late 20th century copy" of the original.[64]

A set of functional items that Mosaic created was to be used on a desk or dresser, all with a theme of dogs. This type of set is sometimes referred to as a dresser caddy or tray. Presumably, the shallow bowl-like bases were for coins or other items men might remove from their pockets and place on their dresser caddy or tray. These items usually have one or two concave bowl-like bases with a dog perched atop the base. The dog breed varies with the tray; some are terriers, Labrador retrievers, or English pointers. Typically, the tray is between 5 and 6 inches tall. The company name is on the bottom or near the dog on the base.

Also possibly used on a desk is a rectangular box with a dog sleeping atop the lid of the box. Another similar dog pose was on a rectangular base with a metal pen holder near the dog's head. Another is a doghouse-shaped box with a sleeping dog on top. Examples of these can be found in classic books by Evan and Louise Purviance, "Zanesville Art Tile in Color," and Wires, Schneider, and Mestre's "Zanesville Decorative Tiles."[65]

The most commonly seen animal figures seen in the "wild" of online auction sites and antique stores are the bison, bear, and two German shepherd dogs. There may be others (in addition to the dogs for use on a desk or dresser mentioned before), but these four are the primary finds. Starting with the bear, this is usually a black bear with subtle

Green tile of elephant on ball (courtesy James Messineo, JMW Gallery).

green glaze in the folds of the bear's fur. Standing on four legs, the bear measures about 6 inches tall and is on a 9.25 inch by 4-inch base. One resource does show this bear in brown and ivory as well.[66]

The American bison, sometimes referred to mistakenly as buffalo (which are indigenous to Asia and Africa), is a formidable animal and in life measures up to 12.5 feet in length and about 2,200 pounds. Perhaps for this reason, the Mosaic Tile bison is the largest of all the animals produced. Identified in many art tile resources, the bison stands approximately 9 inches tall and appears to be at least 11 inches at the base.[67] Featured in white or ivory, the ivory version also has some brown color on the bison and base.

A German shepherd lying on its ceramic base in a creamy brown or light tan color is often found with a second dog in a sitting pose. The two dogs seem to be a pair meant to stay together, but these can be found separately on the antique market. The lying dog is about 6 inches from the tip of its ear to the base and the base is about 11 inches by 3 inches. The dog is marked in a clever spot on the back of the dog's collar with "The Mosaic Tile" in capital letters.

The second dog figurine in sitting position is also usually a creamy brown or tan color but can be found in a dark ivory and a light green color as well. This dog is 9 inches tall from the tip of his ear to the bottom of the base and the base is approximately 7.5 inches by 3 inches. The sitting dog may have the words Mosaic Tile on its collar.

In addition to the dogs and exotic animals, turtles were created for small trinket boxes. The lid of the box was most of the turtle's shell. The turtles were created in various colors and are 1.375 inches tall including the lid, 3.125 inches at the widest part of the front feet, and 4.25 inches from the nose to the tail.

Honorary Memorials

The Company had made at least two busts of well-known Zanesvillians. In 1944, Bethesda Hospital held an event to honor the late William Shinnick, one of the founders of the Mosaic Tile Company and a generous benefactor of the hospital. Shinnick was born on December 21, 1846, and died on May 30, 1923, and this event in 1944 would have marked the 98th anniversary of Shinnick's birth. The Mosaic Tile Company created a "17-inch faience tile plaque bearing a bust of Mr. Shinnick in bas relief."[68] No records can be found of this bust.

A second bust featured Charles (Gene) Griffin, who gained fame as a stunt-flying pilot across the United States, with one world record of 80 turns in a tailspin from a height of 12,000 feet.[69] Griffin's community service focused on helping the returning World War II veterans who wanted to fly after the war and on operating the small Riverside Airport in Zanesville. He died in a flying accident in 1950. In 1952, a "memorial fountain, topped by a bust of Griffin in flight gear, was dedicated at the Municipal Airport."[70] The fountain, the bust, and the plaque were made by Mosaic Tile. During a remodeling at the airport sometime in the 1960s or '70s the bust and plaque were moved inside of the airport office entry.[71]

While not a bust or paperweight, an unusual tile was created in connection to the Knights of Pythias, which also benefited from one of the medallions previously mentioned. This octagonal tile has a green glaze and with measurements of 1.625 inches on the top, bottom, and sides, and the sloping sides are 0.125 inches. The primary image on

Eugene Griffin bust and plaque.

the face of the tile is of O.M. Bake, who was the Grand Chancellor of the Domain of Ohio of the Knights of Pythias.[72] Bake was honored with this tile, presumably, because he was retiring from the Grand Chancellor position in 1907, which is also the year marked on the left side of the tile. Also featured on the tile are the overlapping initials of "KP" for Knights of Pythias, Bake's name impressed on his shirt collar, and "Zanesville" is along the right side.

Fountains

In the 1939 catalog, Mosaic promoted various fountain features.[73] One such fountain "outlet" (from which the water poured) has been saved at the Stone Academy building of the Muskingum County History. According to curator David M. Taylor, this fountain piece was found on one of the outdoor retaining walls of the Academy, being held in place by the rusted remnants of its supply pipe.[74] This was carefully removed and brought into the safety of the museum's showcase. The circular base is piled with shapes of leaves and berries on which is the head and hands of a young blond child. The water of the fountain would have poured over the hands of the figure. Much of the glaze and paint color has been worn away due to time and water. The underside of the fountain has the Mosaic racetrack oval near the middle. A photo of this fountain was also included in the Wires et al. book which mentioned that it was 12 inches in diameter.[75]

Globes

Made in several different color choices, Mosaic's world globe is about 4.25 inches tall with an approximate 3.5-inch base. Most globes are one solid color, but one example found online has been painted and "changed into a polychrome, topographic globe on a base."[76] Another on display at the Olde Town Antique Mall was a tan globe also functioning as a little bank with slit on the top of the globe for coins. Whether that was done by the company or by a globe owner is unknown. The underside of the base is marked with the racetrack oval mark along with the full name of the company and locations of Zanesville and New York.

Cookie Jars

Many pottery companies created cookie jars, and many of the jars depicted a black woman in a long dress, apron, and cap. Often the woman was referred by using the racially insensitive "mammy" or "Aunt Jemima" names. Mosaic Tile was one of the companies that made a cookie jar in this style, and it was the company's only cookie jar. This jar is 13 inches tall and 8 inches across at the base. The circumference of the jar's middle is 21 inches. The jar "is most often wearing a yellow dress with a turban-like headcovering."[77] More difficult to find are the jars with dresses in peach and green, peach and blue, or blue and yellow.[78] The base of the cookie jar is unmarked without any identification of the Mosaic Tile Company. This item has also been on that has been copied or reproduced to fool Mosaic Tile Company collectors.

Bookends.

Bookends

Featured in at least two art pottery resources, the Mosaic Tile bookends feature a young boy reading a book while sitting atop two larger books. Each bookend measures about 7 inches tall with a 4.5-inch base.[79] These were made in ivory and have also been seen in brownish-tan and coppery-black colors.

Stations of the Cross

The path of Jesus Christ starting from where he was condemned to die and leading to the place of his death and entombment has been symbolized in the Stations of the Cross, which is made of 14 images portraying these events.[80] These images have been made in various art forms including out of ceramic tile. According to Jeff Koehler of Koehler Auctions, a set of the Stations of the Cross was designed by Sydney Cope when working at Mosaic Tile.[81] The Cope family was well-known in the Zanesville and Roseville areas, with Sydney's son, Leslie, a prolific and popular artist. Sydney Cope had worked at Mosaic Tile from 1929 through 1934 before he moved to the McCoy Pottery Company.[82]

Up for auction in the spring of 2020, Koehler auctioned and sold 9 of the original 14 stations to 5 different bidders. Each of the station depictions measured 30.5 inches by 20.5 inches and was 3 inches thick. Each was wrapped in a metal frame and backed with plain Mosaic tiles. Each station weighed approximately 20 pounds or more. Each image was made of sculpted clay and individually painted and 8 of the 9 in Koehler's auction had a glossy finish, while the ninth had a matte finish.

While visiting the auction house to view the nine stations, one of Koehler's employees, David A. Briggs indicated that he knew of one additional station tile depiction at the Central Presbyterian Church in Zanesville.[83] Upon contacting the pastor of the church, Tara Mitchell, and a visit to the church, this Station number XII was identical to the other stations in the Koehler auction except the church's had a glossy finish whereas the

Station of the Cross I (courtesy Jeff Koehler, Koehler Auctions).

Station of the Cross IV (courtesy Jeff Koehler, Koehler Auctions).

auction's was in a matte finish. Another source documenting Station XII included the Purviances' book. Station VI was highlighted in the Wires et al. book and was described as "one of 14 faience Stations of the Cross panels made in relief in natural colors, 20" × 30" in size; made also on hand painted panels 9" × 12" in size."[84]

Out of the Ordinary Items

Even harder to find than the giftware are various peripheral items made by the company but possibly not for sale. For example, a photo acquired by Muskingum County History shows the "old pasting room" of the Mosaic Tile Company plant. Taken on April 5, 1955, this photo shows a vast open factory floor space, but upon closer review of the ceiling, a sign hangs down with "VALVE No." painted on it with ivory tiles with painted numbers identifying which valves are attached. The sign is approximately 22 inches long by 4.5 inches high. The tiles are each 3.5 by 3 inches with black numerals. Pre-punched holes are on the top and bottom of each tile for easy attachment. These signs are double-sided with the valve information and tiles repeated. The wood is painted red and the stenciled lettering is white.

When a tile company needed to ship heavy floor tile, what would they use? In the early 1900s, they used wooden shipping boxes. This box is approximately 20 inches in

Mosaic Tile Company factory—valve signs at ceiling (courtesy Muskingum County History).

Valve sign with tile numbers.

Tile numbers.

length and 15 inches in width. The Company name, city, and the oval racetrack mark are on the sides. Only collectors like this author would probably appreciate an old wood box!

In the 1940s and 1950s, employees were provided metal identification badges. These were 2.75 inches by 1.75 inches with a 1.75 by 1.625-inch window for perhaps a photo or other identifying title or numbers and letters combination. Under this window was the racetrack oval impressed on the metal badge. On the back plate of the badge is a metal piece with a large pin marked with a patent number which refers to the work of inventor Henry J. Hanson and approved in 1944.[85] Near the top of the badge, the front and back are attached with a rivet which has the initials "MTC" imprinted on the front, though the initials on most of the badges has been worn off.

How about a service pin for working at the company? A tiny, easy-to-lose pin? Measuring a whopping 0.5 inches, this pin has the oval racetrack logo in the center and the diamond-square base has small decorative marks around the edges. Marked "sterling" on the back with the actual pin mechanism, this little item has thankfully survived.

To know who worked in different offices, name plate tiles were used. These were probably not originally for sale, but about eight names painted on Mosaic Tiles were found in an antique store. On the back of one name plate, Mr. Eugene Hoosan's, the company name was clearly marked with the oval racetrack logo. It appears that a 6 by 6-inch ivory tile may have been used and cut into strips to accommodate the names. This

Mosaic Tile Company wood shipping box.

Identification badge samples.

example is 6 inches by about 1.25 inches with a deep red color used for the name in all capital letters. Mr. Hoosan was also listed in the "Honor Roll" of the Fiftieth Anniversary Program for Mosaic Tile as one of the employees who had served in the U.S. armed forces.[86]

Perhaps attempting to break into the creative crafts market, the Mosaic Tile Company created a box of small tile pieces as a "Hobby Package" for the "home hobbyist" and "leisure time artist" who wanted to create their own mosaic mural.[87] The box of small tiles came without designs, leaving that up to the creative side of the buyer. There is enough tile in the box to cover "about seven square feet … [and] are fadeproof, stain proof, weatherproof, scratchproof and are practically

Employee service pin.

indestructible" so the home hobbyists would need their own chisel, hammer, and nippers to create the shapes they would need for their mosaic design.[88]

Many other unique products have been seen in other respected published sources including a 6 inch "buffalo head in high relief," a tablet with Roman numerals representing the "Ten Commandments," a plaque featuring a lamb and flag with a cross representing the "Lamb of God," and a plaque with Franklin D. Roosevelt's image.[89] A light fixture measuring 3.5 inches by 9.5 inches with multiple bird images and geometric shapes was shown in Sigafoose's book.[90] Wires et al. described a "sunk and raised process" used on tiles that appears to be similar to the "dry line" process described by Sigafoose or possibly a "cuerdo seca" process which uses a wax that "repels the glaze which you then apply to the colored areas. When the wax burns out a black line is left behind."[91]

Name plate sample.

Fraternity plaque (courtesy Muskingum County History).

Without a complete record of all items the company created over the years, some pieces surface with the Mosaic Tile logo or a family story indicating that the company created one item for a special occasion or person. An example of this is a fraternity plaque that had been gifted to the Muskingum County History by a member of the Beta Theta Pi fraternity. Its unusual shape is rectangular but has eight curved "sides." The outer edges are yellow with the featured area in a dark blue or black. On top of that dark field is a shield with red and white sections and a blue area with stars and chevron on top. The piece is 9.5 inches across and 11 inches from top to bottom. Under the shield is a ribbon-like swag with the letters "Kai" which may have been the fraternity's motto or, possibly, secret password. The trademark is on the back, although difficult to see.

These one-of-a-kind items lead to the final question of "What is yet to be discovered of the Mosaic Tile Company?" With hope, any new items that are discovered will not be reproductions but, instead, authentic, and rare items that have been carefully stored in someone's attic. Our only hope of respecting and remembering the craftsmanship of our history for generations to come is to share these pieces with others who appreciate art pottery, history, and the Zanesville, Ohio, area.

Epilogue

This chapter was originally planned to be the "Conclusion," but, I began to realize that this book may end, but the story of the Mosaic Tile Company will not. Even though the buildings are nearly demolished, and the company no longer functions as it had, the memories of the people, whom I have met while researching for this book, are strong and vivid. "My dad used to work there…." "I worked at Mosaic during summers while in college…." "I lived in a house on the street next to the factory…." and "My family had Mosaic Tile walls and floors …." are still fresh stories for the people who live in Zanesville and Muskingum County. In almost every antique store in the southeastern Ohio area, you can find at least one of Mosaic's decorative tiles or trivets.

The legacy of this Company—the entrepreneurship, the innovativeness, the desire for the American dream of prosperity—represents the people of this region of Ohio. Just one look at the progress in the downtown area of Zanesville shows a glimpse of what could be: Old buildings in the process of being restored by artists and small business owners, preserving the history and the beauty of the craftsmanship from long ago. Far too many buildings have already been lost in the last several decades; now is our collective chance to rally around the efforts to save those buildings and ultimately to patronize those businesses that open there.

So, what is next for the Mosaic Tile Company? Maybe a renewed interest in their products? Perhaps. I am hopeful that at the very least, with this resource now available to record and showcase as many of their products as possible, that we will have a renewed appreciation for those tiles that we took for granted and for that artistic ingenuity that we often overlook for something cheaper and easier to access at the local big box store.

Appendix: Compilation of Additional Sites of Installations

Various Mosaic Tile Company works have been noted in records, but not all can be found after all these years. This list is a compilation of these records in an attempt to capture the memory and perhaps shed light on those that are listed.

Source	Date	Site of Installation	City/State
Mosaic Tile Company Catalog	1938	Highland Elementary School	Lynn, Massachusetts
Mosaic Tile Company Catalog	1938	Coca-Cola	Memphis, Tennessee
Mosaic Tile Company Catalog	1938	DePaul Hospital	St. Louis, Missouri
Mosaic Tile Company Catalog	1938	Supreme Food Market	Knoxville, Tennessee
Mosaic Tile Company Catalog	1939	St. Margaret Mary's Church	Chicago, Illinois
Mosaic Tile Company Catalog	1939	Thomas Street Church	Lansing, Michigan
Mosaic Tile Company Catalog	1939	Ottawa Hill Memorial Park Cemetery	Toledo, Ohio
Mosaic Tile Company Catalog	1939	Our Lady of Loretto Church	Philadelphia, Pennsylvania
Mosaic Tile Company Catalog	1939	Albion College	Albion, Michigan
Mosaic Tile Company Catalog	1939	Hi-Speed Service Station	Flint, Michigan
Mosaic Tile Company Catalog	1939	Candyland	Nashville, Tennessee
Mosaic Tile Company Catalog	1939	Laboratory Spaces, Mellon Institute	Pittsburgh, Pennsylvania
Mosaic Tile Company Catalog	1939	Pickwick Landing Dam	Hardin County, Tennessee
Mosaic Tile Company Catalog	1939	East Liberty Presbyterian Church	Pittsburgh, Pennsylvania
Mosaic Tile Company Catalog	1939	Patterson Memorial Pool	Dayton, Ohio
Mosaic Tile Company Catalog	1939	Armstrong Clothing Company	Cedar Rapids, Iowa
Mosaic Tile Company Catalog	1939	Nashua High School	Nashua, New Hampshire
Mosaic Tile Company Catalog	1939	Charity Hospital of Louisiana	New Orleans, Louisiana

Source	Date	Site of Installation	City/State
Mosaic Tile Company Catalog	1939	Menasha School	Menasha, Wisconsin
Sunday Times Signal	September 10, 1944	New Bismarck Hotel	Chicago, Illinois
Mosaic Tile Company 50th Anniversary Program	1944	Subways in several large eastern cities	Unknown
Times Recorder	October 6, 1960	President Eisenhower's Gettysburg and Augusta Homes	Gettysburg, Pennsylvania Augusta, Georgia
Times Recorder	October 6, 1960	Palaces of the Kings of Thailand and Ethiopia	
Times Recorder	October 6, 1960	Hospitals in Korea and Hawaii	
Times Recorder	October 6, 1960	Willow Run Airport	Detroit, Michigan
Times Recorder	October 6, 1960	International Airport	Miami, Florida
Times Recorder	February 4, 1962	South Milwaukee High School	Milwaukee, Wisconsin
Times Recorder	September 17, 1984	Betty Zane Mural at Columbia Gas	Wheeling, West Virginia
Zanesville Decorative Tiles, Wires, Schneider, and Mesre	1972	Roosevelt Mansion at Hyde Park	New York
Zanesville Decorative Tiles, Wires, Schneider, and Mesre	1972	U.S. Army Barracks	Balboa, Canal Zone
Zanesville Decorative Tiles, Wires, Schneider, and Mesre	1972	Charity Hospital	New Orleans
Zanesville Decorative Tiles, Wires, Schneider, and Mesre	1972	Morrison and Sherman Hotels	Chicago
Zanesville Decorative Tiles, Wires, Schneider, and Mesre	1972	Bing Crosby's home	Hollywood
Zanesville Decorative Tiles, Wires, Schneider, and Mesre	1972	Jockey Club	Buenos Aires, Argentina
Zanesville Decorative Tiles, Wires, Schneider, and Mesre	1972	Subways	Philadelphia, Pennsylvania

Chapter Notes

Chapter 1

1. David M. Taylor, "John McIntire and Dr. Increase Mathews: A Comparison of the Founding Fathers of Zanesville" (lecture, Zanesville 1810 Project, Zanesville, Ohio, July 7, 2010).
2. Taylor, "John McIntire."
3. "Putnam and Zanesville: The Story of Two Cities." *Exploring the Ycity*, 18 Sept. 2013, exploringycity.wordpress.com/2013/09/19/putnum-and-zanesville-the-story-of-two-cities/.
4. Elijah Hart Church, "The Early History of Zanesville." *The Zanesville Daily Courier*, 6 July 1878.
5. William M. Corry, "In Commemoration of the Sesquicentennial Anniversary of the Founding of the City of Zanesville." October 3, 1947. Zanesville.
6. Church, "The Early History," 6 July, 1878, 1; Ian Webster, "Inflation Rate between 1800–2020: Inflation Calculator." Accessed August 16, 2020. https://www.officialdata.org/us/inflation/1800?amount=100.
7. Norris F. Schneider, *The McIntire Estate: 1815–1980*. Zanesville, OH: Zanesville Canal and Manufacturing, 1981.
8. Norris F. Schneider, *Y-Bridge City: The Story of Zanesville and Muskingum County, Ohio*. Cleveland, OH: World Publishing Company, 1950.
9. "Putnam and Zanesville: The Story of Two Cities." *Exploring the Ycity*.
10. J. Hope Sutor, *Past and Present of the City of Zanesville and Muskingum County, Ohio*. Chicago, IL: S.J. Clarke Publishing Company, 1905.
11. Schneider, *The McIntire Estate*.
12. Sutor, *Past and Present*.
13. "Putnam and Zanesville: The Story of Two Cities."
14. Sutor, *Past and Present*.
15. Corry, "In Commemoration of the Sesquicentennial."
16. Sutor, *Past and Present*.
17. Sutor, *Past and Present*.
18. Norris F. Schneider, *The Dr. Increase Mathews House: Home of Pioneer and Historical Society of Muskingum County*. Zanesville, OH: N.p., 1975.
19. "Matthews House." n.d. Muskingum County History. Accessed October 24, 2020. http://www.muskingumcountyhistory.org/matthews-house-1.

20. Schneider, *The Dr. Increase Mathews House*.
21. Corry, "In Commemoration of the Sesquicentennial."
22. Taylor, *John McIntire*.
23. Taylor, *John McIntire*.
24. "Muskingum County Ohio." n.d. Muskingum. Accessed January 28, 2019. https://www.muskingumcountyoh.gov/.
25. Norris F. Schneider, *The Famous Y Bridge at Zanesville, Ohio*, 1958
26. "Muskingum County Ohio."
27. "Muskingum County Ohio."
28. "Muskingum County Ohio."
29. "Muskingum County Ohio."
30. "Y Bridge." n.d. "Visit Zanesville Muskingum County Ohio." Muskingum County Convention Visitors Bureau. Accessed January 28, 2019. http://www.visitzanesville.com/Explore/Destinations/175/Y-Bridge/#.
31. "Muskingum County Ohio."
32. "Y Bridge."
33. "Muskingum County Ohio."
34. "Zanesville, Ohio." n.d. Zanesville, Ohio—Ohio History Central. Accessed September 6, 2020. https://ohiohistorycentral.org/w/Zanesville,_Ohio.
35. Elijah Hart Church, "The Early History of Zanesville." *The Zanesville Daily Courier*, 27 April 1878, pp. 1.
36. Schneider, *The McIntire Estate*.
37. Schneider, *The McIntire Estate*.

Chapter 2

1. Ohio Department of Natural Resources, Mark E. Wolfe and Steven D. Blankenbeker. 2005. *Clay and Shale in Ohio*. No. 12.
2. *The Times Recorder*. 1905. "Address by Toastmaster R.L. Quisser," March 17, 1905.
3. Caleb Atwater, *History of the State of Ohio Natural and Civil*. 1838, 2nd ed. Cincinnati, OH: Glezen & Shepard.
4. J. F. Everhart, *1794. History of Muskingum County, Ohio, with Illustrations and Biographical Sketches of Prominent Men and Pioneers*. Columbus, OH: JF Everhart and Co., 1882.
5. Ohio Department of Natural Resources, *Clay and Shale*.

6. Tony Hansen, Digitalfire.com Reference Library, Accessed October 31, 2020. https://digitalfire.com/glossary/buff+stoneware.

7. Anne E. Grimmer, and Kimberly A. Konrad. "Preservation Brief 40: Preserving Historic Ceramic Tile Floors." National Parks Service. October 1996. Accessed February 27, 2019. https://www.nps.gov/tps/how-to-preserve/briefs/40-ceramic-tile-floors.htm.

8. "Raw Clays." Clay Planet—Ceramic Supplies, Clay & Glaze Manufacturer. Accessed October 31, 2020. https://shop.clay-planet.com/rawclay.aspx.

9. Ries, Heinrich, PhD, and Henry Leighton. *History of the Clay-working Industry in the United States*. 1st ed. New York: John Wiley & Sons, 1909.

10. State of Ohio. Seventy-Second General Assembly. *Annual Reports for 1895*. Columbus, OH: Westbote Co., 1896.

11. "Zanesville, Ohio Population 2019." Zanesville, Ohio Population 2019 (Demographics, Maps, Graphs). Accessed August 11, 2019. https://worldpopulationreview.com/us-cities/zanesville-oh-population.

12. Schneider, Norris F., *The Muskingum River: A History and Guide*. Columbus, OH: Ohio Historical Society, 1968.

13. James L. Murphy, *James L. Murphy's Checklist of 19th-Century Bluebird Potters and Potteries in Muskingum County, Ohio*. Edited by Jeff Carskadden and Richard Gartley. Zanesville, OH: Muskingum Valley Archaeological Survey, 2014.

14. State of Ohio, *Annual Reports for 1895*

15. "Ohio Ceramic Center Described in Historical Society Bulletin." *The Times Recorder* (Zanesville), February 14, 1971. Accessed April 5, 2020.

16. Murphy, *James L. Murphy's Checklist*

17. "Muskingum County History Timeline." *The Times Recorder* (Zanesville), February 21, 2005. Accessed August 18, 2020.

18. "Ohio Ceramic Center Described." *The Times Recorder*.

19. Sutor, *Past and Present*.

20. Sutor, *Past and Present*.

21. Sutor, *Past and Present*.

22. "Muskingum County History Timeline." *The Times Recorder*.

23. Stanley E. Wires, Norris F. Schneider, and Moses Mesre. *Zanesville Decorative Tiles*. Zanesville, OH: N.p., 1972.

24. James L. Murphy, and James F. Morton. *Muskingum Bluebirds: A Preliminary Checklist of Nineteenth Century Potters and Potteries in Muskingum County, Ohio*. Columbus, OH: N.p., 1986.

25. Chuck Martin, "A Look at Muskingum County's History." *The Times Recorder* (Zanesville), February 21, 2005. Accessed August 18, 2020.

26. Martin, "A Look at Muskingum County's History"

27. *Roseville's Sesquicentennial*. Roseville 1-5-0 Committee, October 20, 1990. Roseville.

28. *Roseville's Sesquicentennial*. Roseville 1-5-0 Committee.

29. *Roseville's Sesquicentennial*. Roseville 1-5-0 Committee.

30. "J. B. Owens Pottery: A History of the Owens Pottery Company." J. B. Owens Pottery: Antique Zanesville Art Ceramics. 2018. Accessed November 08, 2020. https://owenspottery.com/history.html.

31. "J. B. Owens Pottery." J. B. Owens Pottery.

32. "J. B. Owens Pottery." J. B. Owens Pottery.

33. Ohio Historical Marker. 2007. Roseville Pottery Company: 1890–1957; Linden Avenue Plant, Zanesville.

34. *Roseville's Sesquicentennial*. Roseville 1-5-0 Committee.

35. *Roseville's Sesquicentennial*. Roseville 1-5-0 Committee.

36. Martha Sanford, and Steve Sanford. *Sanfords Guide to Pottery by McCoy*. Campbell, CA: Adelmore Press, 1997.

37. "History: Burley Clay." History. Accessed October 31, 2020. https://burleyclay.com/history/.

38. "History: Burley Clay."

39. Norris F. Schneider, *The History of South Zanesville* (Zanesville: The Times Recorder, 1957), quoted in *South Zanesville, Ohio: Centennial 1890–1990, Souvenir Book* (Zanesville: N.p., 1990).

40. Ron Hoopes, *The Collectors Guide and History of Gonder Pottery: The Other Zanesville, Ohio Art Pottery, with Value Guide*. Gas City, IN: L-W Book Sales, 1992.

41. Hoopes, *The Collector's Guide*.

42. Hoopes, *The Collector's Guide*.

43. Grimmer and Konrad, "Preservation Brief 40."

44. "The American Art Tile, 1880–1940." 2012. Accessed January 18, 2020. http://www.tfaoi.com/aa/10aa/10aa86.htm.

45. Greg Myroth, "Ohio Art Pottery." *Art Pottery Blog*, June 9, 2008. Accessed February 19, 2020. art-potteryblog.com/site/2008/06/ohio-art-potter.html.

Chapter 3

1. Norris F. Schneider, "Karl Langenbeck Helped Establish Mosaic Tile." *The Times Recorder* (Zanesville), March 8, 1970. Accessed April 16, 2020.

2. Herbert Peck, *The Book of Rookwood Pottery*. Cincinnati, OH: Crown Publishing Group, 1968.

3. Schneider, "Karl Langenbeck Helped Establish Mosaic Tile."

4. Schneider, "Karl Langenbeck Helped Establish Mosaic Tile."

5. Schneider, "Karl Langenbeck Helped Establish Mosaic Tile."

6. Stan Jones, "Ceramics Art or Science." Accessed April 22, 2020. https://ceramicsartorscience.co.uk/EicBooks/bookpage.php?eicbookident=caoslive&eicbookpage=308.

7. "The Mosaic Tile Company's Works." *Brick & Clayworker*, Vol. VI, no. 3 (March 1897).

8. Evan Purviance, and Louise Purviance. *Zanesville Art Tile in Color*. Des Moines, IA: Wallace-Homestead Book, 1972.

9. State of Ohio, *Annual Reports for 1895*

10. Wires, Schneider, and Mesre. *Zanesville Decorative Tiles.*

11. "Relief Sculpture." Relief Sculpture: Definition, Types, History. Accessed August 16, 2020. http://www.visual-arts-cork.com/sculpture/relief.htm.

12. Schneider, "Karl Langenbeck Helped Establish Mosaic Tile."

13. Michael Sims, "The Tiles of Zanesville, Ohio: America's Tile Manufacturing Center." *Flash Point,* Vol. 6, No. 3 (July-September 1993): 19.

14. Barbara A. Perry, *American Art Pottery from the Collection of Everson Museum of Art.* New York: Harry N. Abrams, Inc., 1997.

15. Norman Karlson, *American Art Tile: 1876–1941.* New York: Rizzoli, 1998.

16. Lisa Factor Taft, "Herman Carl Mueller (1854–1941), Innovator in the Field of Architectural Ceramics" (PhD diss. Ohio State University, 1979), https://etd.ohiolink.edu/pg_10?0::NO:10:P10_ACCESSION_NUM:osu1487084652613915

17. Schneider, "Karl Langenbeck Helped Establish Mosaic Tile."

18. Herman C. Mueller, Process of and Apparatus for Manufacturing Mosaics. U.S. Patent 537,703, filed April 12, 1894, and issued April 16, 1895.

19. "The New Jersey Mosaic Tile Co., Matawan, N.J." *Brick*, September 1, 1903.

20. Mueller, Process of and Apparatus for Manufacturing Mosaics.

21. Lucile Henzke, *American Art Pottery.* Camden, NJ: T. Nelson, 1970.

22. Ralph M. Kovel, and Terry H. Kovel. *The Kovels' Collectors Guide to American Art Pottery.* New York: Crown, 1974.

23. *Mosaic Tile Company 1894–1944: Fiftieth Anniversary Program.* Zanesville, OH: Mosaic Tile Company, 1944.

24. "The Mosaic Tile Company's Works, Zanesville, O." *Brick,* Vol. VI, no. 3 (March 1897).

25. State of Ohio, *Annual Reports for 1895.*

26. Herman C. Mueller, "Ceramic Mosaic." *The Clay-Worker,* Vol. XXXIX, no. 1 (January 1903).

27. *Mosaic Tile Company 1894–1944: Fiftieth Anniversary Program.*

28. *Mosaic Tile Company 1894–1944: Fiftieth Anniversary Program.*

29. "Historical Sketch of Mosiac [*sic*] Tile Co." *Sunday Times Signal* (Zanesville), October 26, 1943. Accessed December 26, 2019.

30. "Historical Sketch," *Sunday Times Signal.*

31. *Ohio Historic Places Dictionary*, Vol. 2. St. Clair, MI: Somerset Publishers, 1999.

32. "Historical Sketch," *Sunday Times Signal.*

33. "Historical Sketch," *Sunday Times Signal.*

34. *Mosaic Tile Company 1894–1944: Fiftieth Anniversary Program.*

35. Norris F. Schneider, "Mosaic, Largest U.S. Tile Plant, Prepares to Observe 50th Birthday." *Sunday Times Signal* (Zanesville), September 10, 1944. Accessed September 13, 2020.

36. Schneider, "Mosaic, Largest U.S. Tile."

37. Kovel, and Kovel, *The Kovels' Collectors Guide to American Art Pottery.*

38. "Buff Stoneware." Digitalfire.com Reference Library. 2017. Accessed October 20, 2020. https://digitalfire.com/glossary/buff stoneware.

39. "The Mosaic Tile Company's Works." *Brick & Clayworker*, Vol. VI, no. 3 (March 1897).

40. "The Mosaic Tile Company's Works." *Brick & Clayworker.*

41. "Sagger." Dictionary.com. Accessed October 31, 2020. https://www.dictionary.com/browse/sagger.

42. "The New Jersey Mosaic Tile Co., Matawan, N.J." *Brick,* Vol. XIX, no. 3 (September 1, 1903).

43. "The New Jersey Mosaic Tile Co., Matawan, N.J." *Brick.*

44. "The Potteries of Zanesville, Ohio." *The Clay-Worker,* Vol. XXXVII, no. 6 (June 1902). Accessed January 1, 2019.

45. "The New Jersey Mosaic Tile Co., Matawan, N.J." *Brick.*

46. *Mosaic Tile Company 1894–1944: Fiftieth Anniversary Program.*

47. Karl Langenbeck, and Herman C. Mueller, Tile-Setting. U.S. Patent 664,169, filed July 13, 1900, and issued December 18, 1900.

48. Langenbeck, and Mueller. Tile-Setting.

49. *Mosaic Tile Company 1894–1944: Fiftieth Anniversary Program.*

50. Everhart, *1794. History of Muskingum County, Ohio.*

51. Kovel, and Kovel. *The Kovels Collectors Guide to American Art Pottery.*

52. "The New Jersey Mosaic Tile Co., Matawan, N.J." *Brick.*

53. "Historical Sketch," *Sunday Times Signal.*

54. Taft, "Herman Carl Mueller."

55. Schneider, "Karl Langenbeck Helped Establish Mosaic Tile."

56. *Mosaic Tile Company 1894–1944: Fiftieth Anniversary Program.*

57. "William M. Shinnick Educational Fund." William M. Shinnick Educational Fund. Accessed March 4, 2020. https://www.shinnickeducationalfund.com/About-William-M-Shinnick-Educational-Fund-Muskingum-County-Ohio/.

58. Sutor, *Past and Present.*

59. Sutor, *Past and Present.*

60. "Historical Sketch," *Sunday Times Signal.*

61. "Historical Sketch," *Sunday Times Signal.*

62. *Mosaic Tile Company 1894–1944: Fiftieth Anniversary Program.*

63. "Historical Sketch," *Sunday Times Signal.*

64. *Mosaic Tile Company 1894–1944: Fiftieth Anniversary Program.*

65. *Mosaic Tile Company 1894–1944: Fiftieth Anniversary Program.*

66. Susan Mussi, "Ceramic–Pottery Dictionary." Accessed August 16, 2020. http://ceramicdictionary.com/en/m/414/mill.

67. *Mosaic Tile Company 1894–1944: Fiftieth Anniversary Program.*

68. *Mosaic Tile Company 1894–1944: Fiftieth Anniversary Program.*

69. "March 23–27, 1913: Statewide Flood." Accessed September 19, 2020. http://ohsweb.ohiohistory.org/swio/pages/content/1913_flood.htm.

70. Cliff Pinkard, "Researchers Trying to Put Flood of 1913 Back in Public's Consciousness on Its 100th Anniversary." Cleveland.com. March 22, 2013. Accessed November 18, 2019. Cleveland.com/metro/index.ssf/2013/03/researchers_trying_to_put_floo.html.

71. "March 23–27, 1913: Statewide Flood."

72. *Mosaic Tile Company 1894–1944: Fiftieth Anniversary Program.*

73. *Mosaic Tile Company 1894–1944: Fiftieth Anniversary Program.*

74. Henzke, *American Art Pottery.*

75. Sanford, and Sanford. *Sanfords' Guide to Pottery by McCoy.*

76. Norris F. Schneider, "Floor Tile Made Here Is Still in Use Nationwide." *The Times Recorder* (Zanesville), May 28, 1972. Accessed January 18, 2019.

77. Ralph M. Kovel, and Terry H. Kovel. *Kovels' American Art Pottery.* New York: Crown Publishers, 1993.

78. *Mosaic Tile Company 1894–1944: Fiftieth Anniversary Program.*

79. MacGhille-Eoin McLean, "The Spanish Flu: A Footnote to WWI." The Spanish Flu: A Footnote to WWI. March 4, 2019. http://mccogs.blogspot.com/2019/03/the-spanish-flu-footnote-to-wwi.html.

Chapter 4

1. "Engineering Properties of Historic Brick: Variability Considerations as a Function of Stationary and Nonstationary Kiln Types." *Journal of the American Institute for Conservation,* Vol. 43, no. 3 (2004). Accessed May 5, 2020.

2. "Engineering Properties of Historic Brick." *Journal of the American Institute for Conservation.*

3. "Growth of Mosaic Tile Co. from Small Beginning Has Been Wonderful." *The Times Recorder* (Zanesville), September 4, 1919. Accessed February 5, 2019.

4. Sanford, and Sanford. *Sanfords' Guide to Pottery by McCoy.*

5. "Growth of Mosaic Tile Co.," *The Times Recorder.*

6. "Growth of Mosaic Tile Co.," *The Times Recorder.*

7. Tile Terms Glossary. Accessed September 22, 2020. https://www.tilemountain.co.uk/tile_terms_glossary.

8. Henzke, *American Art Pottery.*

9. "Growth of Mosaic Tile Co.," *The Times Recorder.*

10. "Growth of Mosaic Tile Co.," *The Times Recorder.*

11. "Growth of Mosaic Tile Co.," *The Times Recorder.*

12. *Mosaic Tile Company 1894–1944: Fiftieth Anniversary Program.*

13. "Historical Sketch," *Sunday Times Signal.*

14. "Antique Gloss Black Mosaic Tile Company Box Cap Molding Bathroom Tile." The Period Bath Supply Company (A Division of Historic Houseparts, Inc.). Accessed May 4, 2020. https://www.periodbath.com/antique-gloss-black-mosaic-tile-Company-box-cap-molding-bathroom-tile.html.

15. "Sagger." Dictionary.com.

16. "Mosaic Tile Company Records: Collection Synopsis." Accessed December 28, 2018. https://www.ohiomemory.org/digital/collection/aids/id/6080.

17. *Mosaic Tile Company 1894–1944: Fiftieth Anniversary Program.*

18. "William M. Shinnick," William M. Shinnick Educational Fund.

19. "William M. Shinnick," William M. Shinnick Educational Fund.

20. Norris F. Schneider, "Scholarship Funds Available for Students Here." *The Times Recorder* (Zanesville), April 1, 1973. Accessed March 24, 2019.

21. "William M. Shinnick," William M. Shinnick Educational Fund.

22. *Mosaic Tile Company 1894–1944: Fiftieth Anniversary Program.*

23. *Mosaic Tile Company 1894–1944: Fiftieth Anniversary Program*; Ralph M. Kovel, and Terry H. Kovel. *Kovels' American Art Pottery.*

24. Kovel, and Kovel. *The Kovels' Collectors Guide to American Art Pottery.*

25. Kovel, and Kovel. *The Kovels' Collectors Guide to American Art Pottery.*

26. *Mosaic Tile Company 1894–1944: Fiftieth Anniversary Program.*

Chapter 5

1. "The Cost of Living in the 1930s." Accessed September 22, 2020. https://sites.google.com/site/thecostoflivinginthe1930s/#:~:text=In the 1930s.

2. "Great Depression History." History.com. February 28, 2020. Accessed September 22, 2020. http://www.history.com/topics/great-depression/great-depression-history.

3. "The Cost of Living in the 1930s."

4. *Mosaic Tile Company 1894–1944: Fiftieth Anniversary Program..*

5. *Mosaic Tile Company 1894–1944: Fiftieth Anniversary Program.*

6. Schneider, "Floor Tile Made Here."

7. Schneider, "Floor Tile Made Here."

8. "What Is the Difference between Overglaze and Underglaze?" DPH Trading. Accessed September 22, 2020. https://www.dphtrading.com/customer-service/guides/tips-and-ideas/what-is-the-difference-between-overglaze-und-underglaze#:~text=in the case of.

9. "What Is the Difference between Overglaze and Underglaze?" DPH Trading.

10. "Historical Sketch." *Sunday Times Signal.*

11. Schneider, "Mosaic, Largest U.S. Tile."

12. Mosaic Tile Company. *Hand Book of Mosaic Clay-Tiles*. Zanesville, Ohio: Mosaic Tile Company, 1939.

13. Mosaic Tile Company. *Hand Book of Mosaic Clay-Tiles*.

14. *Mosaic Tile Company 1894–1944: Fiftieth Anniversary Program*.

15. *Mosaic Tile Company 1894–1944: Fiftieth Anniversary Program*.

16. "Mosaic Tile Co. Is Largest Firm of Its Kind in Country." *The Times Recorder*, October 2, 1947. Accessed March 22, 2019.

17. Norris F. Schneider, *Zanesville Art Pottery*. Zanesville, OH: N.p., 1963.

18. Betty Purviance Ward, and Nancy N. Schiffer. *Weller, Roseville & Related Zanesville Art Pottery & Tiles*. Atglen, PA: Schiffer Publishing, 2000.

19. George D. Ford, and Otto T. Kauffmann. Electrically-Conductive Ceramic Floor-Tile Units and Floors Composed of Such Conductive Units. U.S. Patent 2,851,639, filed March 27, 1952, and issued September 9, 1958.

20. Ford, and Kauffmann. Electrically-Conductive Ceramic Floor-Tile Units.

21. "Mosaic Tile ... Now on Duty in New Good Samaritan Hospital Addition, Too." *The Times Recorder* (Zanesville), December 12, 1956. Accessed March 24, 2019.

22. "Mosaic Tile Ready to Meet Expected Boom in Building." *The Times Recorder* (Zanesville), June 22, 1957. Accessed March 24, 2019.

23. Herbert G. Macdonald, David J. Barbour, and Karl M. Claus. Multiple Unit Ceramic Tile Assembly. U.S. Patent US3041785A, filed January 9, 1959, and issued July 3, 1962.

24. Macdonald, Barbour, and Claus. Multiple Unit Ceramic Tile.

Chapter 6

1. "Mosaic Opens New Warehouse in Tennessee." *The Times Recorder* (Zanesville), October 17, 1960. Accessed September 27, 2020.

2. Herbert G. Macdonald, David J. Barbour, Karl M. Claus, and Robert B. Cleverly. Method of Fabricating a Multiple Unit Assembly. U.S. Patent 3,185,748, filed January 27, 1961, and issued May 25, 1965.

3. Macdonald, Barbour, and Claus. Multiple Unit Ceramic Tile Assembly.

4. Macdonald, Barbour, Claus, and Cleverly. Method of Fabricating a Multiple Unit Assembly.

5. "Illness Mystery Probed at Mosaic Tile Plant." *The Times Recorder* (Zanesville), April 5, 1962. Accessed February 17, 2020.

6. "Illness Mystery Probed." *The Times Recorder*.

7. Kat Escher, "The Story of the Real Canary in the Coal Mine." Smart News. December 30, 2016. Accessed May 10, 2020. https://www.smithsonianmag.com/smart-news/story-real-canary-coal-mine-180961570/.

8. Escher, "The Story of the Real Canary."

9. "Illness Mystery Probed." *The Times Recorder*.

10. "Mosaic Tile Promotes Two Executives Here." *The Times Recorder* (Zanesville), August 11, 1962. Accessed September 27, 2020.

11. United States Tariff Commission. *Tariff Commission Reports to the President on Ceramic Mosaic Tile Workers' Petition for Adjustment Assistance*. Washington, DC, 1963.

12. United States Tariff Commission. *Tariff Commission Reports*.

13. "Mosaic Tile to Close Pershing Road Plant." *The Times Recorder* (Zanesville), October 28, 1966. Accessed February 5, 2019.

14. "Mosaic Tile to Close." *The Times Recorder*.

15. "Some Mosaic Assets Sold by Marmon." *The Times Recorder* (Zanesville), April 27, 1968. Accessed February 5, 2019.

16. "Mosaic Reaffirms Plant Closing." *The Times Recorder* (Zanesville), March 24, 1967. Accessed January 28, 2019.

17. "Mosaic Reaffirms Plant Closing." *The Times Recorder*.

18. Newell Harvey, "Businessman Purchase [*sic*] Mosaic Facilities Here." *The Times Recorder* (Zanesville), June 17, 1967. Accessed March 24, 2019.

19. Harvey, "Businessman Purchase."

20. Harvey, "Businessman Purchase."

21. "Some Mosaic Assets Sold by Marmon." *The Times Recorder*.

22. "Old Roseville Pottery Property to Be Sold at Auction June 27." *The Times Recorder* (Zanesville), June 12, 1968. Accessed March 24, 2019.

23. "Old Roseville Pottery Property." *The Times Recorder*.

Chapter 7

1. "Some Mosaic Assets Sold by Marmon." *The Times Recorder*.

2. "Tile Firm Acquired by Stylon." *The Morning Call* (Allentown), May 5, 1968. Accessed September 20, 2020; "Mosaic Identifies Takeover Leaders." *The Times Recorder* (Zanesville), February 22, 1967. Accessed September 20, 2020.

3. "Infill—Bright Idea That Became a Disaster." *The Boston Globe* (Boston), August 24, 1975. Accessed October 31, 2020.

4. "Infill—Bright Idea." *The Boston Globe*.

5. "Muskingum County GIS." *Muskingum County Auditor*. Accessed December 26, 2018. http://www.muskingumcountyauditor.org.

6. Muskingum County. Recorder's Office. *Grant Index to Deeds—Muskingum County, Ohio—Grantors*. Record Vol. 596. Page 103. August 1971.

7. Gene L. MacDonald, "Former Tile Properties Utilized." *The Times Recorder* (Zanesville), April 25, 1972. Accessed March 24, 2019.

8. MacDonald, "Former Tile Properties Utilized."

9. Schneider. "Floor Tile Made Here."

10. Muskingum County. Recorder's Office.

Assignment and Assumption Agreement. Vol. 10. Page 188. April 1977

11. Muskingum County. Recorder's Office. *Assignment and Assumption.*

12. Muskingum County. Recorder's Office. Satisfaction of Mortgage. 194th ed. Vol. 945. September 1986.

13. Muskingum County. Recorder's Office. Affidavit. Book 1601. Page 542. August 2001.

14. Muskingum County. Recorder's Office. Limited Warranty Deed. Book 1778. Page 181. June 2003.

15. Chris Crook, "Attorney General Files Suit against Former Lear Property Owners, including Catfish LLC." *The Times Recorder* (Zanesville), June 1, 2020. Accessed September 28, 2020.

16. Crook. "Attorney General Files Suit."

17. Telephone interview by author with Jay Bennett. February 15, 2019.

18. Chris Crook, "ZFD Found Burning Pallet in Vacant Building." *The Times Recorder* (Zanesville), January 30, 2020. Accessed September 28, 2020.

19. Muskingum County. Auditor. Tax Data. Zanesville, OH, 2018. Parcel 82-27-01-04-000

20. Muskingum County. Auditor. Tax Data.

21. Muskingum County. Recorder's Office. Online Land Records. Zanesville, OH, 2003–2017.

22. "Sheriff's Sale of Real Estate." *The Times Recorder* (Zanesville), January 22, 2019. Accessed May 16, 2020.

23. E-mail interview by author with Jodi Moody. May 18, 2020.

24. E-mail interview by author with Kristin D. Baughman. May 26, 2020.

25. E-mail interview by author with Dr. Elizabeth Kline. May 15, 2020.

26. *VAP Phase I Property Assessment.* Report. Zanesville, Ohio: SME, 2017. Project Number 074522.00.04A.002 Senior Consultant Keith B. Egan

27. *VAP Phase I Property Assessment.*

28. *VAP Phase I Property Assessment.*

29. *VAP Phase I Property Assessment.*

30. *VAP Phase I Property Assessment.*

31. *VAP Phase I Property Assessment.*

32. "Mosaic Tile Dumpsite Focus of Cleanup." *American Recycler.* May 2003. Accessed December 25, 2018. http://www.americanrecycler.com/may2003/mosaic.html.

33. Peggy Matthews, "Lead Danger Is Found Here." *The Times Recorder* (Zanesville), August 16, 1991. Accessed May 16, 2020.

34. *2015 Groundwater Monitoring Report.* Project no. 21–18216A. United States Environmental Protection Agency, Region 5 and Ohio Environmental Protection Agency. Ch, IL: Ramboll Environ, 2017.

35. Matthews. "Lead Danger Is Found Here."

36. "Mosaic Tile Dumpsite Focus of Cleanup." *American Recycler.*

37. Brad Stimple, *Mosaic Tile Dump Site Operable Unit (OU) 1.* EPA OSC Response. Ohio Environmental Protection Agency. Zanesville, OH, 2020.

38. Stimple. *Mosaic Tile Dump Site.*

39. Stimple. *Mosaic Tile Dump Site.*

40. *2015 Groundwater Monitoring Report.* Ohio Environmental Protection Agency.

41. *Summer 2013 Groundwater Monitoring Report.* Project no. 21–18216A. United States Environmental Protection Agency, Region 5 and Ohio Environmental Protection Agency. Chicago, IL: ENVIRON International Corporation, 2013.

42. *Summer 2013 Groundwater Monitoring Report.* U.S. Environmental Protection Agency.

43. *Summer 2013 Groundwater Monitoring Report.* U.S. Environmental Protection Agency.

44. *2015 Groundwater Monitoring Report.* Ohio Environmental Protection Agency.

45. "Long-Term Assessment Monitoring Mosaic Tile Dump." Kevin O'Hara to Brad Stimple. October 22, 2019. U.S. EPA Region 5, Westlake, Ohio.

46. City of Zanesville, Ohio. *Community Visioning & Planning Session—We Want Your Input!* May 14, 2016. PowerPoint Presentation, Zanesville.

47. Online interview by author with Mayor Donald L. Mason. May 14, 2020.

48. Online interview by author with Mayor Donald Mason.

49. "Land Reutilization Corporation." Muskingum County, Ohio. 2020. Accessed May 14, 2020. https://www.muskingumcountyoh.gov/Muskingum-County-Land-Reutilization-Corporation/.

50. Email interview by author with Andy Roberts, September 4, 2020.

51. Online interview by author with Mayor Donald Mason.

Chapter 8

1. Sutor, *Past and Present.*

2. Sutor, *Past and Present.*

3. Barbara J. Starbuck, "Mission Possible: Preservationists Want to Turn Garfield into Museum, Community Gathering Place." *The Times Recorder* (Zanesville), December 10, 1991. Accessed October 3, 2020.

4. Patrick Jackson, "Restoring Garfield Will Be Labor of Love." *The Times Recorder* (Zanesville), December 10, 1997. Accessed October 3, 2020.

5. Jackson. "Restoring Garfield."

6. Peggy Matthews, "Historic Garfield Razed, but Memories Linger on." *The Times Recorder* (Zanesville), April 17, 2001. Accessed October 3, 2020.

7. Beth Rickett, "Memories Remain Though Schools Are Gone." *The Times Recorder* (Zanesville), April 23, 1990. Accessed October 3, 2020.

8. Norris F. Schneider, *St. Nicholas Catholic Church.* August 23, 1959. Zanesville, Ohio.

9. Schneider. *St. Nicholas Catholic Church.*

10. Schneider. *St. Nicholas Catholic Church.*

11. Purviance, and Purviance. *Zanesville Art Tile in Color.*

12. "Landing of Columbus." Architect

of the Capitol. Accessed October 31, 2020. https://www.aoc.gov/explore-capitol-campus/art/landing-columbus.

13. Schneider. *St. Nicholas Catholic Church.*

14. Beth Rickett, "Hotel Rogge." *The Times Recorder* (Zanesville), April 9, 1990. Accessed March 22, 2019.

15. Rickett. "Hotel Rogge."

16. Rickett. "Hotel Rogge."

17. "Mosaic Tile." *The Times Recorder* (Zanesville), November 27, 1899. Accessed August 30, 2020.

18. "Mosaic Tile." *The Times Recorder.*

19. Rickett. "Hotel Rogge."

20. Norris F. Schneider, "Dedication of New County Home Wing to Occur Today." *The Times Recorder* (Zanesville), March 11, 1973, sec. D. Accessed October 4, 2020.

21. Schneider. "Dedication of New County Home."

22. "Brief Mention." *The Times Recorder* (Zanesville), June 15, 1900. Accessed August 30, 2020.

23. "Historic Register Accepts Adena Court Apartments." *The Times Recorder* (Zanesville), November 12, 1980. Accessed February 21, 2019.

24. "Lenhart Mansion Walls Are Found during Renovation of Apartments." *The Times Recorder* (Zanesville), December 10, 1990. Accessed February 21, 2019.

25. "Historic Register Accepts Adena." *The Times Recorder.*

26. Norris F. Schneider, *History of Zanesville High School.* Zanesville, OH: Creative Graphics of Ohio, 1988.

27. Thomas W. Lewis, "History of Zanesville and Muskingum County." *The Times Recorder* (Zanesville), September 27, 1924. Accessed November 10, 2019.

28. Lewis. "History of Zanesville and Muskingum County."

29. Schneider. *History of Zanesville High School.*

30. Norris F. Schneider, "Second Campaign for $500,000 Is Needed to Complete Construction of YMCA Here." *The Times Recorder* (Zanesville), April 16, 1961. Accessed May 20, 2020.

31. Schneider. "Second Campaign."

32. "Cornerstone of the New 'Y' Will Be of Mosaic Tile." *The Times Recorder* (Zanesville), September 11, 1919. Accessed May 20, 1919.

33. "Rotary Reporter: Shuffleboard Is a Teen-age Hit." *The Rotarian,* January 1951.

34. "New Idea in Recreation—All-Tile, Outdoor Shuffleboard!" *The Mountain Echo* (Shickshinny, PA), March 9, 1951. Accessed January 28, 2019.

35. "New Idea in Recreation." *The Mountain Echo.*

36. "Peoples Savings Bank Will Keep Open House Two Days." *The Times Recorder* (Zanesville), August 4, 1926. Accessed February 24, 2019.

37. Kathryn Lynch, and Michael S. Sims. *Zanesville.* Charleston, SC: Arcadia, 2005.

38. "Chronology of Zanesville and Vicinity." *The Times Recorder* (Zanesville), December 30, 1940. Accessed May 20, 2020.

39. History.com Editors. "Works Progress Administration (WPA)." History.com. July 13, 2017. Accessed May 8, 2020. http://www.history.com/topics/great-depression/works-progress-administration.

40. "Materials Used in Auditorium Reach Astronomical Figures." *The Times Recorder* (Zanesville), April 15, 1940. Accessed January 12, 2019.

41. "3-Day ZTC Starts Today." *The Times Recorder* (Zanesville), June 16, 1978. Accessed November 27, 2019.

42. Norris F. Schneider, "Tile Mural in New Auditorium Symbolizes Growth of City." *The Zanesville Daily,* May 19, 1940. Accessed January 2019.

43. "Secrest Auditorium and Music Hall." Zanesville, Ohio—Secrest Auditorium and Music Hall—About—Eents [*sic*]. 2019. Accessed January 12, 2019. https://www.secrestauditorium.com/About/.

44. "Williams Delicatessen." *The Times Recorder* (Zanesville), October 2, 1947. Accessed February 12, 2019.

45. "Williams Delicatessen." *The Times Recorder.*

46. "Commercial Supply Co. Formal Opening Saturday." *The Times Recorder* (Zanesville), November 21, 1947. Accessed March 22, 2019.

47. "Learning, Living, Growing with Christ as Our Leader." St. John's Lutheran Church. May 5, 2014.

48. "Learning, Living, Growing with Christ." St. John's Lutheran Church.

49. "Baker Chapel Is Memorial to the Late Albert T. Baker." *The Times Recorder* (Zanesville), June 17, 1950. Accessed February 1, 2019.

50. "Learning, Living, Growing with Christ." St. John's Lutheran Church.

51. "Crown, Cross & Crown, and IHS." St. Mark's Evangelical Lutheran Church. Accessed October 3, 2020. http://www.stmarkshsv.org/symbols-crowncrossihs.html.

52. "Learning, Living, Growing with Christ." St. John's Lutheran Church.

53. Mona Culver, "Mosaic Gains National Prominence in Architectural Designing Field." *The Times Recorder* (Zanesville), January 28, 1951. Accessed February 1, 2019.

54. "Taylor Gets Contract for New Building." *The Times Recorder* (Zanesville), February 12, 1959. Accessed May 20, 2020.

55. Kathie Pratt, "Profiles: Of People and the Times." *The Times Recorder* (Zanesville), May 12, 1968. Accessed November 27, 2019.

56. "Swimming Pool Opened at Country Club." *The Times Recorder* (Zanesville), August 31, 1953. Accessed February 1, 2019.

57. "To Break Ground for Swim Pool." *The Times Recorder* (Zanesville), May 25, 1953. Accessed January 31, 2019.

58. "To Break Ground for Swim Pool." *The Times Recorder.*

59. Norris F. Schneider, "Penney Closing Ends Era in Downtown Zanesville." *The Times Recorder* (Zanesville), November 2, 1980. Accessed October 3, 2020.

60. "Modern Store Building Is Penney's Pre-Christmas Gift to Zanesville." *The Times Recorder* (Zanesville), November 4, 1953. Accessed May 17, 2019.

61. "Modern Store Building." *The Times Recorder.*

62. Schneider. "Penney Closing Ends Era."

63. "We Congratulate." *The Times Recorder* (Zanesville), June 12, 1954. Accessed May 17, 2019.

64. "We Congratulate." *The Times Recorder.*

65. "We Congratulate." *The Times Recorder.*

66. "Historic Headley Inn Bed and Breakfast." Historic Headley Inn. 2018. Accessed October 31, 2020. https://headleyinn.com/about.

67. "Use Mosaic Tile in New Building." *The Times Recorder* (Zanesville), May 19, 1955. Accessed May 17, 2019.

68. "Use Mosaic Tile in New Building." *The Times Recorder.*

69. Mary Ann Bucci, *Stories & Art.* Zanesville, OH: N.p., 2015.

70. "Question: When Is a Door Not a Door?" *The Times Recorder* (Zanesville), June 4, 1955. Accessed March 22, 2019.

71. "Construction of First Trust Building OKd." *The Times Recorder* (Zanesville), February 7, 1975. Accessed October 4, 2020.

72. "The History of Genesis." Genesis HealthCare System. Accessed May 9, 2020. https://www.genesishcs.org/about-us/history/.

73. "Mosaic Tile ... Now on Duty in New Good Samaritan Hospital Addition, Too." *The Times Recorder* (Zanesville), December 12, 1956. Accessed March 24, 2019.

74. "Mosaic Tile ... Now on Duty." *The Times Recorder.*

75. "Mosaic Tile ... Now on Duty." *The Times Recorder.*

76. "The History of Genesis." Genesis HealthCare System.

77. "This Morning's Paper Printed at New Plant." *The Times Recorder* (Zanesville), September 27, 1926. Accessed February 24, 2019.

78. "Tile Mural Unveiled on New Building." *The Times Recorder* (Zanesville), October 3, 1958. Accessed February 24, 2019.

79. "Tile Mural Unveiled on New Building." *The Times Recorder.*

80. Muskingum County. Auditor. Property Data. Zanesville, OH, 2020. Parcel 81-65-02-09-000

81. Lorena England, and Phyllis Thompson. *A History of Faith United Methodist Church.* Zanesville, OH: N.p., 1984.

82. *Specifications of the Materials and Labor to Be Used and Employed in the Erection of First Evangelical United Brethren Church.* Cambridge, OH: Sigman & Tribbie, Registered Architects, 1959.

83. *Specifications of the Materials and Labor.* Sigman & Tribbie.

84. England and Thompson. *A History of Faith United Methodist Church.*

85. Muskingum Watershed Conservancy District. "Great Flood of 1913 Led to MWCD, System of Dams and Reservoirs." March 24, 2013. Accessed January 18, 2019. https://www.mwcd.org/news/2013/03/24/great-flood-of-1913-led-to-mwcd-system-of-dams-and-reservoirs.

86. "Dillon Dam to Be Dedicated This Afternoon." *The Times Recorder* (Zanesville), October 2, 1960. Accessed November 10, 2019.

87. "A Sermon Written on the Face of the Land..." *The Times Recorder* (Zanesville), September 30, 1960. Accessed November 10, 2019.

88. "A Sermon Written on the Face of the Land..." *The Times Recorder.*

89. Anna Rumer, "Bloomer Candy Production Moves." *The Times Recorder* (Zanesville), May 21, 2014. Accessed October 4, 2020.

90. "Clossman Hardware Store." Landmark Hunter.com. August 16, 2016. Accessed November 15, 2020. https://landmarkhunter.com/182878-clossman-hardware-store/.

91. "Clossman Unique Market." Facebook. Accessed May 26, 2020. https://www.facebook.com/Clossman-Unique-Market-104137651151466.

92. Chris Crook, "The Rebirth of a Downtown Icon." *The Times Recorder* (Zanesville), March 5, 2020. Accessed October 4, 2020.

93. Interview by author with Paul Emory. May 26, 2020.

94. "Purchased Main Street Shop." *The Times Recorder* (Zanesville), December 3, 1949. Accessed October 7, 2020.; "629 Main St." *Times Signal* (Zanesville), March 27, 1959. Accessed October 4, 2020.

95. *Zanesville Official City Directory and Complete Classified Business and Professional Directory, 1910.* Akron, OH: Burch Directory, 1909.

96. Jim Rudloff, "Department Store Nears End of Its Era." *The Times Recorder* (Zanesville), February 6, 1997. Accessed October 5, 2020.

97. Rudloff. "Department Store Nears End."

98. Black-Elliott Block. May 2017. Accessed February 2, 2019. https://ipfs.io/ipfs/QmXoypizjW 3WknFiJnKLwHCnL72vedxjQkDDP1mXWo6uco/wiki/Black-Elliott_Block.html.

99. Interview by author with Jeffrey Snyder. May 22, 2020.

100. "Coca-Cola Is America's Fun Drink." *The Times Recorder* (Zanesville), August 20, 1960. Accessed May 22, 2020.

101. "Ohio Soft Drink Bottling Plants: RoadsideArchitecture.com." Ohio Soft Drink Bottling Plants | RoadsideArchitecture.com. Accessed January 7, 2019. https://www.roadarch.com/beverage/oh.html.

102. Karlson. *American Art Tile: 1876–1941.*

103. "Ohio Soft Drink Bottling Plants." RoadsideArchitecture.com

104. Norris F. Schneider, "Building Was Only 31 Years Old." *The Times Recorder* (Zanesville), January 20, 1963. Accessed February 25, 2019.

105. Schneider. "Building Was Only 31 Years Old."

106. Schneider. "Building Was Only 31 Years Old."

107. Schneider. "Building Was Only 31 Years Old."

108. "To Combine the City Hall with Market House." *The Times Recorder* (Zanesville), February 10, 1914. Accessed February 25, 2019.

109. Beth Rickett, "Fourth Street Building Houses Many Different Businesses over the Years." *The Times Recorder* (Zanesville), August 13, 1990. Accessed February 24, 2019.

110. Rickett. "Fourth Street Building."

111. *Zanesville Official City Directory and Complete Classified Business and Professional Directory, 1924.* Akron, OH: Burch Directory Company, 1923.

112. *Zanesville Official City Directory and Complete Classified Business and Professional Directory, 1926–27.* Akron, OH: Burch Directory Company, 1926.

113. *Zanesville Official City Directory and Complete Classified Business and Professional Directory, 1928–29.* Akron, OH: Burch Directory Company, 1928.

Chapter 9

1. "Muskingum River." Muskingum River—Ohio History Central. Accessed March 9, 2019. http://ohiohistorycentral.org/w/Muskingum_River.

2. Dylan Taylor-Lehman, "The Ups and Downs of Being a Canal Lockmaster." Atlas Obscura. August 15, 2018. Accessed March 9, 2019. https://www.atlasobscura.com/articles/river-canal-lock-master.

3. "U.S. Engineer Office." *Marietta Daily Leader* (Marietta), April 6, 1899. Accessed March 9, 2019.; "Lockmaster's House Historical Marker." Historical Marker. May 08, 2017. Accessed March 9, 2019. https://www.hmdb.org/m.asp?m=103279.

4. E-mail interview by author with David M. Taylor. October 20, 2020.

5. "Mural for Conservancing [*sic*] District." *The Times Recorder* (Zanesville), June 3, 1958. Accessed October 8, 2020.

6. "Mural for Conservancing [*sic*] District." *The Times Recorder.*

7. E-mail interview by author with Karen Miller. August 25, 2020.

8. "Souvenir Program: Dedication Noble County Court House." Ohio Memory Collection. 1934. Accessed April 26, 2020. https://ohiomemory.org/digital/collection/p267401coll36/id/15488.

9. "Souvenir Program." Ohio Memory Collection.

10. "Souvenir Program." Ohio Memory Collection.

11. "Finest of Its Kind." *The Times Recorder* (Zanesville), December 3, 1898. Accessed August 30, 2020.

12. "Finest of Its Kind." *The Times Recorder.*

13. Mosaic Tile Company. *Mosaic Tile Catalog.* Zanesville, Ohio, 1938.

14. Mosaic Tile Company. *Mosaic Tile Catalog.* Zanesville, Ohio, 1938.

15. John Harper, "5 Things to Know about St. Thomas Hospital, Where Security Guard Was Stabbed Tuesday." Cleveland.com. February 17, 2016. Accessed October 1, 2020. https://www.cleveland.com/akron/2016/02/five_things_to_know_about_st_t.html.

16. "The Great Seal of California." California State Seal—California State Symbols and Emblems. Accessed May 25, 2020. https://www.netstate.com/states/symb/seals/ca_seal.htm.

17. "State Capitol—Eureka Tiles." California State Capitol Museum in Sacramento, California. Accessed April 17, 2020. http://capitolmuseum.ca.gov/architecture-and-history/architectural-virtual-tour.

18. "The Great Seal of California."

19. "The Great Seal of California."

20. Michele Grimm, and Tom Grimm. "Restoration Returns Glory to State Capitol." *Los Angeles Times.* December 13, 1987. Accessed November 15, 2020. https://www.latimes.com/archives/la-xpm-1987-12-13-tr-28324-story.html.

21. Jennifer Heit, "On Round Ground." March 12, 1995. Accessed March 16, 2019. https://www.sun-sentinel.com/news/fl-xpm-1995-03-12-9503160192-story.html.

22. Heit. "On Round Ground."

23. "Kennan Building—Dan Duckham Architect: Organic Architectural Design Services," Dan Duckham Architect | Organic Architectural Design Services, 1991, |PAGE|, accessed March 16, 2019, http://www.danduckham.com/kennan-building

24. Blair Kamin, "1927 Athletic Club Proves Fit for Luxury Apartments." Chicagotribune.com. March 07, 2014. Accessed October 9, 2020. https://www.chicagotribune.com/news/ct-xpm-2014-03-07-ct-met-athleticclub-20140307-story.html.

25. "Late 1920's Original and Intact Polychromatic Lakeshore Drive Athletic Club Glazed Red Clay Interior Pool Room Figural 'clam Shell' Wall Tile." Urban Remains. Accessed January 7, 2019. https://www.urbanremainschicago.com/late-1920-s-original-and-intact-polychromatic-lakeshore-drive-athletic-club-glazed-red-clay-interior-pool-room-figural-clam-shell-wall-tile.html.

26. "Late 1920's Original and Intact." Urban Remains.

27. "Late 1920's Original and Intact." Urban Remains.

28. Peter Strazzabosco, "Union Park Hotel Approved for Landmark Status." City of Chicago: Union Park Hotel Approved for Landmark Status. June 9, 2010. Accessed May 25, 2020. https://www.chicago.gov/city/en/depts/dcd/provdrs/hist/news/2010/mar/union_park_hotelproposedforlandmarkstatus.html.

29. Mosaic Tile Company. *Mosaic Tile Catalog.* Zanesville, Ohio, 1938.

30. United States Department of the Interior. National Park Service. National Register of Historic Places Registration Form. Chicago, IL, 2010.

31. "Building, Chapel, & Library." Disciples Divinity House, University of Chicago, Accessed May 25, 2020. https://ddh.uchicago.edu/about/building-chapel-library/.

32. Mosaic Tile Company. *Mosaic Tile Catalog.* Zanesville, Ohio, 1938.

33. "Coca-Cola to Greet Public on Thursday Eve." *The Call-Leader* (Elwood), May 31, 1938. Accessed May 25, 2020.

34. Donald D. Doxsee, "A Walking Tour of the Allen County Courthouse." Fort Wayne, 2005.

35. Georgiana W. Bond, and Ada C. Fenton, *Guide to Allen County Court House,* 1953.

36. Doxsee. "A Walking Tour of the Allen County Courthouse."

37. *Mosaic Tile Company 1894–1944: Fiftieth Anniversary Program.*

38. "The Beginning Years." Henry Ford Health System. Accessed May 25, 2020. https://www.henryford.com/about/culture/history/hfhs/beginning.

39. "The Beginning Years." Henry Ford Health Systems.

40. "Breakthrough Treatments and Delivery." Henry Ford Health System. Accessed May 25, 2020. https://www.henryford.com/about/culture/history/hfhs/breakthrough.

41. Sharon Sanders, "The Art of Printing." SeMissourian.com. February 28, 2013. Accessed May 25, 2020. https://www.semissourian.com/blogs/fromthemorgue/entry/51580.

42. Sanders. "The Art of Printing."

43. "Pace-Setter Home Theme of Talk." *The Times Recorder* (Zanesville), May 8, 1951. Accessed September 23, 2020.

44. Ian Webster, " Inflation Rate between 1635-2020: Inflation Calculator." U.S. Inflation Calculator: 1635→2020, Department of Labor Data. Accessed September 23, 2020. https://www.in2013dollars.com/us/inflation.; "Walleisa Has Fabrics from Pace-setter House for 'House Beautiful.'" Pottsville Republican (Pottsville), May 3, 1951. Accessed September 23, 2020.

45. "Pace-Setter House for 1951." *Tampa Bay Times* (St. Petersburg), September 9, 1951. Accessed September 23, 2020.

46. "Pace-Setter Home Theme of Talk." *The Times Recorder.*

47. Culver. "Mosaic Gains National Prominence."

48. Culver. "Mosaic Gains National Prominence."

49. Culver. "Mosaic Gains National Prominence."

50. Culver. "Mosaic Gains National Prominence."

51. Culver. "Mosaic Gains National Prominence."

52. *Mosaic Tile Company 1894–1944: Fiftieth Anniversary Program.*

53. "Holland Tunnel: Facts & Info." The Port Authority of New York and New Jersey Holland Tunnel. Accessed July 20, 2019. https://www.panynj.gov/bridges-tunnels/en/holland-tunnel/facts-info.html.

54. *Titusville Historic Walking Tour.* PDF. Titusville. https://visitcrawford.org/wp-content/uploads/2019/01/HIstoric-Titusville-Walking-Tour-2014-compressed.pdf

55. Jessica Hilburn, "The Colonel Drake Hotel." NWPA Stories. August 22, 2018. Accessed May 25, 2020. https://nwpastories.com/2018/22/the-colonel-drake-hotel/.

56. "Penney's Salutes Mosaic Tile!" *The Times Recorder* (Zanesville), October 6, 1960. Accessed December 26, 2019.

57. Hilburn. "The Colonel Drake Hotel."

58. "See the Mosaic Display at Penney's!" *The Times Recorder.*

59. Hilburn. "The Colonel Drake Hotel."

60. *Titusville Historic Walking Tour.* PDF. Titusville.

61. Mosaic Tile Company. *Mosaic Tile Catalog,* Zanesville, Ohio, 1938.

62. Mosaic Tile Company. *Mosaic Tile Catalog,* Zanesville, Ohio, 1938.

63. Mosaic Tile Company. *Mosaic Tile Catalog,* Zanesville, Ohio, 1938.

64. "Will Rogers Memorial Center's Coliseum and Auditorium Tile Murals." Fort Worth Public Art. Accessed May 7, 2020. https://fwpublicart.org/will-rogers/.

65. "Part of a Ceramic-tile Mural by Works Project Administration Artist Kenneth Gale, Depicting Texas History, at the Will Rogers Auditorium, Now Part of the Will Rogers Memorial Center in Fort Worth, Texas." The Library of Congress. October 2012. Accessed May 7, 2020. https://www.loc.gov/item/2013650766.

66. "Rotarians to Hear Well Known Artist." *The Zanesville Signal,* March 28, 1938. Accessed November 17, 2020.

67. "Part of a Ceramic-tile Mural by Works Project." The Library of Congress.

68. "Will Rogers Memorial Center's Coliseum." Fort Worth Public Art.

69. Alex Boyer, "Fort Worth Art Commission Votes to Leave Will Rogers Mural Intact, Add Historical Context." FOX 4 News Dallas-Fort Worth. January 22, 2020. Accessed May 7, 2020. https://www.fox4news.com/news/fort-worth-art-commission-votes-to-leave-will-rogers-mural-intact-add-historical-context.

70. Grimmer, and Konrad. "Preservation Brief 40."

71. Grimmer, and Konrad. "Preservation Brief 40"

72. "National Building Museum–Washington, DC." MDT Travels. Accessed March 14, 2019. https://www.moderndaytripper.com/national-building-museum-washington-dc/.

73. Grimmer, and Konrad. "Preservation Brief 40"

74. "National Building Museum." MDT Travels.

75. Sally Sims Stokes, "Documenting the History of the White House Library Fireplace Tiles, 1944–1962." *Art Documentation: Journal of the*

Art Libraries Society of North America 36, no. 1 (2017): 50–72. Accessed January 18, 2020. doi:10.1086/691372.

76. Stokes, "Documenting the History."

77. Stokes, "Documenting the History."

78. "History of the Mary H. Weir Public Library." Mary H. Weir Public Library. Accessed November 29, 2019. http://www.weirton.lib.wv.us/hancock/weir/maryhweir/history.html.

79. Charles Dietz, "Letter to the Editor: Zanesville's Grand Young Man of Art." *The Times Recorder* (Zanesville), September 17, 1984. Accessed October 10, 2020.; "History of the Mary H. Weir." Mary H. Weir Public Library.

80. "History of the Mary H. Weir Public Library." Mary H. Weir Public Library.

81. "Panama Canal." History.com. August 04, 2015. Accessed May 25, 2020. https://www.history.com/topics/landmarks/panama-canal.

82. "Panama Canal." History.com.

83. Ira Elbert Bennett, *History of the Panama Canal: Its Construction and Builders.* Washington, DC: Historical Publishing Co., 1915.

84. Bennett. *History of the Panama Canal.*

85. Bennett. *History of the Panama Canal.*

86. Bennett. *History of the Panama Canal.*

87. Daniel Funke, "A Timeline of the Panama Canal." *Los Angeles Times.* June 24, 2016. Accessed October 10, 2020. https://www.latimes.com/world/mexico-americas/la-fg-panama-canal-timeline-20160622-snap-htmlstory.html.

88. "Mosaic Products on Luxury Liner America." *The Times Recorder* (Zanesville), January 5, 1940. Accessed May 19, 2019.

89. "The SS *America*: The Many Lives of a Great Ship." S.S. *America*, S.S. *United States* Sailing on the 'All American' Team to Europe. August 31, 1939. Accessed May 7, 2020. http://united-states-lines.org/history-2/.

90. "Mosaic Products on Luxury Liner *America*." *The Times Recorder.*

91. "Mosaic Products on Luxury Liner *America*." *The Times Recorder.*

92. "Mosaic Products on Luxury Liner *America*." *The Times Recorder.*

93. "The Story of the S.S. *America*." Sometimes Interesting. June 27, 2011. Accessed May 25, 2020. https://sometimes-interesting.com/2011/06/27/the-ss-america/.

94. "The Story of the S.S. *America*." Sometimes Interesting.

95. "The Story of the S.S. *America*." Sometimes Interesting.

96. "S. S. Zanesville." *The Times Recorder* (Zanesville), December 8, 1944. Accessed August 30, 2020.

97. "S.S. *Zanesville*." *The Times Recorder*

98. Chuck Martin, "S.S. *Zanesville* Launched with Great Fanfare." *The Times Recorder* (Zanesville), January 26, 2002. Accessed October 10, 2020.; Sims, Michael. "OH_Zanesville––S.S. *Zanesville* Victory Ship Plaque." Historic U.S. Tile Installations, O–W. November 2010. Accessed October 4, 2020. https:// sites.google.com/site/tileinstallationdatabasemz/oh_zanesville—s-s-zanesville-victory-ship-plaque.

Chapter 10

1. Kovel, and Kovel. *The Kovels' Collectors Guide to American Art Pottery.*

2. Dick Sigafoose, *American Art Pottery: Identification & Values.* 2nd ed. Paducah, KY: Collector Books, 2006.

3. Chad Lage, *Pictorial Guide to Pottery & Porcelain Marks.* Paducah, KY: Collector Books, 2004.

4. Wires, Schneider, and Mesre. *Zanesville Decorative Tiles*; Lehner, Lois. *Ohio Pottery and Glass: Marks and Manufacturers.* Des Moines, IA: Wallace-Homestead Book, 1978.

5. *Zanesville Official City Directory and Complete Classified Business and Professional Directory.* Akron, OH: Burch Directory Company, 1939.

6. Purviance and Purviance. *Zanesville Art Tile in Color.*

7. Mosaic Tile Company. *Hand Book of Mosaic Clay-Tiles,* 1939.

8. Mosaic Tile Company. *Hand Book of Mosaic Clay-Tiles.*

9. Mosaic Tile Company. *Mosaic Tile Company Catalog,* Derby, Connecticut, 1949.

10. Perry, *American Art Pottery.*

11. Perry, *American Art Pottery.*

12. Edward FitzGerald, trans. *Rubáiyát of Omar Khayyám.* London: Arcturus Publishing Limited, 2018.

13. "Decorated Hot Plates Available to Employees." *The Mosaic Times*, November 1958.

14. "Decorated Hot Plates Available to Employees." *The Mosaic Times.*

15. "Rare Mosaic Tile Co 1930–1964 Vintage Pottery Turquoise Tray." EBay. Accessed August 30, 2020. https://www.ebay.com/itm/RARE-MOSAIC-TILE-CO-1930-1964-VINTAGE-POTTERY-TURQUOISE-TRAY/360534282135?hash=item53f1848f97:g:mu4AAOxy-1lRHpP9.

16. Purviance and Purviance. *Zanesville Art Tile in Color.*

17. "Mosaic Tile Co Zanesville OH Pottery Coaster Set—Zanesville Banks Premium." EBay. Accessed November 27, 2020. https://www.ebay.com/itm/284095222986?ul_noapp=true.

18. "Mosaic Tile Co Zanesville OH Pottery Coaster Set—Zanesville Banks Premium." EBay.

19. Mosaic Tile Company. *Hand Book of Mosaic Clay-Tiles.*

20. Mosaic Tile Company. *Mosaic Tile Catalog,* 1938.

21. Mosaic Tile Company. *Mosaic Tile Catalog,* 1938.

22. Trip Gabriel, "Ashtrays: Up in Smoke." *Tampa Bay Times*, September 30, 2005. Accessed August 30, 2020. https://www.tampabay.com/archive/1997/01/18/ashtrays-up-in-smoke/.

23. Sarah Loff, "Sputnik, the Dawn of the Space

Age." NASA. October 04, 1957. Accessed August 30, 2020. https://www.nasa.gov/image-feature/oct-4-1957-sputnik-the-dawn-of-the-space-age.

24. "Vintage Mosaic Tile Company, Zanesville Ohio & New York NY Advertising Ashtray." Worthpoint. Accessed October 12, 2020. https://www.worthpoint.com/worthopedia/vintage-mosaic-tile-Company-434757468.

25. "Col. Spangler Honored: Aide De Camp for K.T. Parade—Mosaic Tiling Co's. Generosity." *The Zanesville Signal*, October 5, 1899. Accessed March 2, 2020.

26. "Col. Spangler Honored." *The Zanesville Signal*.

27. "Antique Tiles." Knights Templar Medallion by Mosaic W/ Ribbon (Stove Tiles and Portrait Tiles) at Antique Tiles. Accessed May 29, 2020. https://www.tias.com/9513/PictPage/1921851682.html.

28. Sigafoose. *American Art Pottery: Identification & Values*.

29. "Grand Lodge Home Page." Home Page. July 8, 2019. Accessed November 2, 2020. http://www.ioofgrandlodgeofohio.org/.

30. Norris F. Schneider, *Bethesda, Your Hospital*. Zanesville, OH: Bethesda Hospital Association, 1965.

31. Nate Harris, "Trustees Trying to Get Rid of Elks Lodge Building." *The Times Recorder* (Zanesville), January 10, 2019. Accessed November 2, 2020.

32. Sigafoose. *American Art Pottery: Identification & Values*.

33. Alan Cuthbertson, "History of Wedgwood Jasper." Collecting Wedgwood. May 15, 2017. Accessed May 30, 2020. https://collectingwedgwood.com/wedgwood-jasper.

34. Michael Padwee, "Tile Back Views." *Flash Point*, January/June 1993.

35. Michael Padwee, "Architectural Tiles, Glass and Ornamentation In New York." December 1, 2016. Accessed April 2, 2020. https://tilesinnewyork.blogspot.com/2016.

36. Padwee. "Architectural Tiles, Glass"

37. Padwee. "Architectural Tiles, Glass"

38. Padwee. "Architectural Tiles, Glass"

39. "Descendants of Founders of New Jersey." Descendants of the Founders of New Jersey Home. Accessed May 27, 2020. https://www.njfounders.org/.

40. "Descendants of Founders of New Jersey." Descendants of the Founders of New Jersey Home.

41. "José Martí." Biography.com. March 23, 2016. Accessed May 29, 2020. https://www.biography.com/writer/jose-marti.

42. "Simón Bolívar." Biography.com. August 18, 2014. Accessed May 29, 2020. https://www.biography.com/political-figure/simon-bolivar.

43. "Simón Bolívar." Biography.com.

44. "Rosario, Argentina." Encyclopædia Britannica. Accessed October 11, 2020. https://www.britannica.com/place/Rosario-Argentina.

45. "History—David Lloyd George." BBC. Accessed May 29, 2020. http://www.bbc.co.uk/history/historic_figures/george_david_lloyd.shtml.

46. "Tile and Mantel Dealers to Meet." *The Buffalo Commercial*, January 24, 1916. Accessed October 11, 2020.

47. Sigafoose. *American Art Pottery: Identification & Values*.

48. "What Is a Billiken?" Saint Louis University. Accessed May 30, 2020. https://www.slu.edu/about/key-facts/what-is-a-billiken.php.

49. " Facebook Post. January 4, 2019. Accessed January 4, 2019. https://www.facebook.com/MuskingumCountyHistory/photos/p.10156749751716605/?type=3&theater.

50. "Royal Order Of Jesters National Court, 002 Pittsburgh Court in Pittsburgh, Pennsylvania (PA)." NonProfitFacts.com—Tax-Exempt Organizations. Accessed May 30, 2020. http://www.nonprofitfacts.com/PA/Royal-Order-Of-Jesters-National-Court-002-Pittsburgh-Court.html.

51. "Political Tiles from the Mosaic Tile Co." Cowan's Auction House.

52. "Sebaugh-Basehart Wedding Today." *The Times Recorder* (Zanesville), June 28, 1911. Accessed November 2, 2020.

53. "Traffic and Transportation." *Electric Railway Journal*, April 2, 1910, 641. Accessed November 2, 2020.

54. "Traffic and Transportation." *Electric Railway Journal*.

55. Greg Daugherty, "General Pershing's Run for President Was a Sure Thing––Until His Troops Spoke Up." History.com. May 23, 2018. Accessed March 31, 2020. https://www.history.com/news/john-j-pershing-presidential-campaign-world-war-i.

56. "Legion Starts New Home Building Fund Selling Local Tile." *The Times Recorder* (Zanesville), August 20, 1929." Accessed May 30, 2020.

57. "Legion Starts New Home Building Fund Selling Local Tile." *The Times Recorder*.

58. "Political Tiles from the Mosaic Tile Co., Zanesville, Ohio, Group of 7, Including Washington, Franklin, Lincoln, & More." Cowan's Auction House: Accessed April 2, 2020. https://www.cowanauctions.com/lot/political-tiles-from-the-mosaic-tile-co-zanesville-ohio-group-of-7-including-washington-franklin-lincoln-more-173240.

59. "Political Tiles from the Mosaic Tile Co." Cowan's Auction House.

60. "J. B. Owens Pottery: A History of the Owens Pottery Company." J. B. Owens Pottery: Antique Zanesville Art Ceramics. 2018. Accessed November 8, 2020. https://owenspottery.com/history.html.; "History of J.B. Owens: J.B Owens Pottery.com." JB Owens Pottery. July 19, 2015. Accessed November 1, 2020. http://www.jbowenspottery.com/history-of-j-b-owens/.

61. Sigafoose. *American Art Pottery: Identification & Values*.

62. *Mosaic Tile Company 1894–1944: Fiftieth Anniversary Program*.

63. Kovel and Kovel. *The Kovels' Collectors Guide to American Art Pottery*.

64. "Mosaic Tile Co 5" × 5" Elephant Advertising Tile Copy Matte Green Arts & Crafts." EBay. Accessed November 8, 2020. https://www.ebay.com/itm/324353721001.

65. Purviance and Purviance. *Zanesville Art Tile in Color*; Wires, Schneider, and Mesre. *Zanesville Decorative Tiles*.

66. Purviance and Purviance. *Zanesville Art Tile in Color*.

67. Purviance and Purviance. *Zanesville Art Tile in Color*.

68. "Hospital Ceremony to Honor Memory of W.M. Shinnick." *Sunday Times Signal* (Zanesville), December 17, 1944. Accessed February 24, 2019.

69. Chuck Martin, "Gene Griffin Was a Record-Setting Flyer." *The Times Recorder* (Zanesville), October 21, 1995. Accessed November 14, 2019.

70. Martin. "Gene Griffin Was a Record-Setting Flyer."

71. Martin. "Gene Griffin Was a Record-Setting Flyer."

72. "All Is in Readiness for Great Convention." *The Times Recorder* (Zanesville), June 8, 1907. Accessed November 2, 2020.

73. Mosaic Tile Company. *Hand Book of Mosaic Clay-Tiles*.

74. Interview by author with David M. Taylor. January 25, 2019.

75. Wires, Schneider, and Mesre. *Zanesville Decorative Tiles*.

76. Padwee, "Architectural Tiles, Glass."

77. Helaine Fendelman, and Joe Rosson. "Mammy Cookie Jar Likely a Reproduction." *Daily Herald* (Chicago), January 23, 2012. Accessed January 7, 2019. https://www.dailyherald.com/article/20120123/entlife/701239931/.

78. Fendelman, and Rosson. "Mammy Cookie Jar Likely a Reproduction."

79. Purviance, and Purviance. *Zanesville Art Tile in Color*; Wires, Schneider, and Mesre. *Zanesville Decorative Tiles*.

80. "Stations of the Cross." Encyclopædia Britannica. April 23, 2020. Accessed July 11, 2020. https://www.britannica.com/print/article/144045.

81. Interview by author with Jeff Koehler. July 11, 2020.

82. Kovel and Kovel. *The Kovels' Collectors Guide to American Art Pottery*.

83. Interview by author with Dave Briggs. July 11, 2020.

84. Wires, Schneider, and Mesre. *Zanesville Decorative Tiles*.

85. Henry J. Hanson, Identification Badge. U.S. Patent 2,341,773, filed September 13, 1940, and issued February 15, 1944.

86. *Mosaic Tile Company 1894–1944: Fiftieth Anniversary Program*.

87. "Mosaic Has Hobby Package." *The Times Recorder* (Zanesville), April 26, 1958. Accessed May 31, 2020.

88. "Mosaic Has Hobby Package." *The Times Recorder*.

89. Purviance and Purviance. *Zanesville Art Tile in Color*.

90. Sigafoose. *American Art Pottery: Identification & Values*.

91. Wires, Schneider, and Mesre. *Zanesville Decorative Tiles*; "Cuerda Seca or Decorating with Black Lines: Big Ceramic Store." BigCeramic Store.com. Accessed November 21, 2020. https://bigceramicstore.com/pages/info-ceramics-tips-tip74_cuerda_seca.

Bibliography

"All Is in Readiness for Great Convention." *The Times Recorder* (Zanesville), June 8, 1907. Accessed November 2, 2020.

"The American Art Tile, 1880–1940." 2012. Accessed January 18, 2020. http://www.tfaoi.com/aa/10aa/10aa86.htm.

"Antique Tiles." Knights Templar Medallion by Mosaic W/ Ribbon (Stove Tiles and Portrait Tiles) at Antique Tiles. Accessed May 29, 2020. https://www.tias.com/9513/PictPage/1921851682.html.

Atwater, Caleb. *History of the State of Ohio Natural and Civil.* 2nd ed. Cincinnati, OH: Glezen & Shepard, 1838.

"Baker Chapel Is Memorial to the Late Albert T. Baker." *The Times Recorder* (Zanesville), June 17, 1950. Accessed February 1, 2019.

"The Beginning Years." Henry Ford Health System. Accessed May 25, 2020. https://www.henryford.com/about/culture/history/hfhs/beginning.

Bennett, Ira Elbert. *History of the Panama Canal: Its Construction and Builders.* Washington, D.C.: Historical Publishing Co., 1915.

Black-Elliott Block. May 2017. Accessed February 2, 2019. https://ipfs.io/ipfs/QmXoypizjW3WknF iJnKLwHCnL72vedxjQkDDP1mXWo6uco/wiki/Black-Elliott_Block.html.

Bond, Georgiana W., and Ada C. Fenton. *Guide to the Allen County Court House.* Fort Wayne, IN: N.p., 1953.

Boyer, Alex. "Fort Worth Art Commission Votes to Leave Will Rogers Mural Intact, Add Historical Context." FOX 4 News Dallas-Fort Worth. January 22, 2020. Accessed May 7, 2020. https://www.fox4news.com/news/fort-worth-art-commission-votes-to-leave-will-rogers-mural-intact-add-historical-context.

"Breakthrough Treatments and Delivery." Henry Ford Health System. Accessed May 25, 2020. https://www.henryford.com/about/culture/history/hfhs/breakthrough.

"Brief Mention." *The Times Recorder* (Zanesville), June 15, 1900. Accessed August 30, 2020.

Bucci, Mary Ann. *Stories & Art.* Zanesville, OH: N.p., 2015.

"Buff Stoneware." Digitalfire.com Reference Library. 2017. Accessed October 20, 2020. https://digitalfire.com/glossary/buff stoneware.

"Building, Chapel, & Library." Disciples Divinity House. Accessed May 25, 2020. https://ddh.uchicago.edu/about/building-chapel-library/.

"Chronology of Zanesville and Vicinity." *The Times Recorder* (Zanesville), December 30, 1940. Accessed May 20, 2020.

Church, Elijah Hart. "The Early History of Zanesville." *The Zanesville Daily Courier,* 27 April 1878, pp. 1–1.

———. "The Early History of Zanesville." *The Zanesville Daily Courier,* 6 July 1878, pp. 1–1.

City of Zanesville, Ohio. *Community Visioning & Planning Session—We Want Your Input!* May 14, 2016. PowerPoint Presentation, Zanesville.

"Clossman Hardware Store." LandmarkHunter.com. August 16, 2016. Accessed November 15, 2020. https://landmarkhunter.com/182878-clossman-hardware-store/.

"Clossman Unique Market." Facebook. Accessed May 26, 2020. https://www.facebook.com/Clossman-Unique-Market-104137651151466.

"Coca-Cola Is America's Fun Drink." *The Times Recorder* (Zanesville), August 20, 1960. Accessed May 22, 2020.

"Coca-Cola to Greet Public on Thursday Eve." *The Call-Leader* (Elwood), May 31, 1938. Accessed May 25, 2020.

"Col. Spangler Honored: Aide De Camp for K.T. Parade—Mosaic Tiling Co's. Generosity." *The Zanesville Signal,* October 5, 1899. Accessed March 2, 2020.

"Commercial Supply Co. Formal Opening Saturday." *The Times Recorder* (Zanesville), November 21, 1947. Accessed March 22, 2019.

"Construction of First Trust Building OKd [sic]." *The Times Recorder* (Zanesville), February 7, 1975. Accessed October 4, 2020.

"Cornerstone of the New 'Y' Will Be of Mosaic Tile." *The Times Recorder* (Zanesville), September 11, 1919. Accessed May 20, 1919.

Corry, William M. *In Commemoration of the Sesquicentennial Anniversary of the Founding of the City of Zanesville.* October 3, 1947. Zanesville.

"The Cost of Living in the 1930s." Google Sites. Accessed September 22, 2020. https://sites.google.com/site/thecostoflivinginthe1930s/#:~:text=In the 1930s.

Crook, Chris. "Attorney General Files Suit against

Former Lear Property Owners, including Catfish LLC." *The Times Recorder* (Zanesville), June 1, 2020. Accessed September 28, 2020.

———. "The Rebirth of a Downtown Icon." *The Times Recorder* (Zanesville), March 5, 2020. Accessed October 4, 2020.

———. "ZFD Found Burning Pallet in Vacant Building." *The Times Recorder* (Zanesville), January 30, 2020. Accessed September 28, 2020.

"Crown, Cross & Crown, and IHS." St. Mark's Evangelical Lutheran Church. Accessed October 3, 2020. http://www.stmarkshsv.org/symbols-crowncrossihs.html.

"Cuerda Seca or Decorating with Black Lines: Big Ceramic Store." BigCeramicStore.com. Accessed November 21, 2020. https://bigceramicstore.com/pages/info-ceramics-tips-tip74_cuerda_seca.

Culver, Mona. "Mosaic Gains National Prominence in Architectural Designing Field." *The Times Recorder* (Zanesville), January 28, 1951. Accessed February 1, 2019.

Cuthbertson, Alan. "History of Wedgwood Jasper." Collecting Wedgwood. May 15, 2017. Accessed May 30, 2020. https://collectingwedgwood.com/wedgwood-jasper.

Daugherty, Greg. "General Pershing's Run for President Was a Sure Thing––Until His Troops Spoke Up." History.com. May 23, 2018. Accessed March 31, 2020. https://www.history.com/news/john-j-pershing-presidential-campaign-world-war-i.

"Decorated Hot Plates Available to Employees." *The Mosaic Times,* November 1958.

"Descendants of Founders of New Jersey." Descendants of the Founders of New Jersey Home. Accessed May 27, 2020. https://www.njfounders.org/.

Dietz, Charles. "Letter to the Editor: Zanesville's Grand Young Man of Art." *The Times Recorder* (Zanesville), September 17, 1984. Accessed October 10, 2020.

"Dillon Dam to Be Dedicated This Afternoon." *The Times Recorder* (Zanesville), October 2, 1960. Accessed November 10, 2019.

"Engineering Properties of Historic Brick: Variability Considerations as a Function of Stationary and Nonstationary Kiln Types." *Journal of the American Institute for Conservation* 43, no. 3 (2004). Accessed May 5, 2020.

England, Lorena, and Phyllis Thompson. *A History of Faith United Methodist Church.* Zanesville, OH: N.p., 1984.

Escher, Kat. "The Story of the Real Canary in the Coal Mine." *Smart News.* December 30, 2016. Accessed May 10, 2020. https://www.smithsonianmag.com/smart-news/story-real-canary-coal-mine-180961570/.

Everhart, J. F. 1794. *History of Muskingum County, Ohio, with Illustrations and Biographical Sketches of Prominent Men and Pioneers.* Columbus, OH: JF Everhart and Co., 1882.

Fendelman, Helaine, and Joe Rosson. "Mammy Cookie Jar Likely a Reproduction." *Daily Herald* (Chicago), January 23, 2012. Accessed

January 7, 2019. https://www.dailyherald.com/article/20120123/entlife/701239931/.

"Finest of Its Kind." *The Times Recorder* (Zanesville), December 3, 1898. Accessed August 30, 2020.

FitzGerald, Edward, trans. *Rubaiiyait of Omar Khayyaim.* London: Arcturus Publishing Limited, 2018.

Ford, George D., and Otto T. Kauffmann. Electrically-Conductive Ceramic Floor-Tile Units and Floors Composed of Such Conductive Units. US Patent 2,851,639, filed March 27, 1952, and issued September 9, 1958.

Funke, Daniel. "A Timeline of the Panama Canal." *Los Angeles Times.* June 24, 2016. Accessed October 10, 2020. https://www.latimes.com/world/mexico-americas/la-fg-panama-canal-timeline-20160622-snap-htmlstory.html.

Gabriel, Trip. "Ashtrays: Up in Smoke." *Tampa Bay Times,* September 30, 2005. Accessed August 30, 2020. https://www.tampabay.com/archive/1997/01/18/ashtrays-up-in-smoke/.

"Grand Lodge Home Page." Home Page. July 8, 2019. Accessed November 2, 2020. http://www.ioofgrandlodgeofohio.org/.

"Great Depression History." History.com. February 28, 2020. Accessed September 22, 2020. http://www.history.com/topics/great-depression/great-depression-history.

Grimm, Michele, and Tom Grimm. "Restoration Returns Glory to State Capitol." *Los Angeles Times.* December 13, 1987. Accessed November 15, 2020. https://www.latimes.com/archives/la-xpm-1987-12-13-tr-28324-story.html.

Grimmer, Anne E., and Kimberly A. Konrad. "Preservation Brief 40: Preserving Historic Ceramic Tile Floors." National Parks Service. October 1996. Accessed February 27, 2019. https://www.nps.gov/tps/how-to-preserve/briefs/40-ceramic-tile-floors.htm.

"Growth of Mosaic Tile Co. from Small Beginning Has Been Wonderful." *The Times Recorder* (Zanesville), September 4, 1919. Accessed February 5, 2019.

Hanson, Henry J. Identification Badge. US Patent 2,341,773, filed September 13, 1940, and issued February 15, 1944.

Harper, John. "5 Things to Know about St. Thomas Hospital, Where Security Guard Was Stabbed Tuesday." Cleveland.com. February 17, 2016. Accessed October 1, 2020. https://www.cleveland.com/akron/2016/02/five_things_to_know_about_st_t.html.

Harris, Nate. "Trustees Trying to Get Rid of Elks Lodge Building." *The Times Recorder* (Zanesville), January 10, 2019. Accessed November 2, 2020.

Harvey, Newell. "Businessman Purchase Mosaic Facilities Here." *The Times Recorder* (Zanesville), June 17, 1967. Accessed March 24, 2019.

Heit, Jennifer. "On Round Ground." March 12, 1995. Accessed March 16, 2019. https://www.sun-sentinel.com/news/fl-xpm-1995-03-12-9503160192-story.html.

Henzke, Lucile. *American Art Pottery*. Camden, NJ: T. Nelson, 1970.

Hilburn, Jessica. "The Colonel Drake Hotel." NWPA Stories. August 22, 2018. Accessed May 25, 2020. https://nwpastories.com/2018/22/the-colonel-drake-hotel/.

"Historic Headley Inn Bed and Breakfast." Historic Headley Inn. 2018. Accessed October 31, 2020. https://headleyinn.com/about.

"Historic Register Accepts Adena Court Apartments." *The Times Recorder* (Zanesville), November 12, 1980. Accessed February 21, 2019.

"Historical Sketch of Mosiac [*sic*] Tile Co." *Sunday Times Signal* (Zanesville), October 26, 1943. Accessed December 26, 2019.

"History: Burley Clay." Accessed October 31, 2020. https://burleyclay.com/history/.

"The History of Genesis." Genesis HealthCare System. Accessed May 9, 2020. https://www.genesishcs.org/about-us/history/.

"History of J.B. Owens: J.B. Owens Pottery.com." JB Owens Pottery. July 19, 2015. Accessed November 1, 2020. http://www.jbowenspottery.com/history-of-j-b-owens/.

"History of the Mary H. Weir Public Library." Mary H. Weir Public Library. Accessed November 29, 2019. http://www.weirton.lib.wv.us/hancock/weir/maryhweir/history.html.

"History—David Lloyd George." BBC. Accessed May 29, 2020. http://www.bbc.co.uk/history/historic_figures/george_david_lloyd.shtml.

"Holland Tunnel: Facts & Info." The Port Authority of New York and New Jersey Holland Tunnel. Accessed July 20, 2019. https://www.panynj.gov/bridges-tunnels/en/holland-tunnel/facts-info.html.

Hoopes, Ron. *The Collectors Guide and History of Gonder Pottery: The Other Zanesville, Ohio-Art Pottery, with Value Guide*. Gas City, IN: L-W Book Sales, 1992.

"Hospital Ceremony to Honor Memory of W.M. Shinnick." *Sunday Times Signal* (Zanesville), December 17, 1944. Accessed February 24, 2019.

"Illness Mystery Probed at Mosaic Tile Plant." *The Times Recorder* (Zanesville), April 5, 1962. Accessed February 17, 2020.

"Infill—Bright Idea That Became a Disaster." *The Boston Globe*, August 24, 1975. Accessed October 31, 2020.

"J. B. Owens Pottery: A History of the Owens Pottery Company." J. B. Owens Pottery: Antique Zanesville Art Ceramics. 2018. Accessed November 08, 2020. https://owenspottery.com/history.html.

Jackson, Patrick. "Restoring Garfield Will Be Labor of Love." *The Times Recorder* (Zanesville), December 10, 1997. Accessed October 3, 2020.

Jones, Stan. "Ceramics Art or Science." Ceramics. Accessed April 22, 2020. https://ceramicsartorscience.co.uk/EicBooks/bookpage.php?eicbookident=caoslive&eicbookpage=308.

"José Martí." Biography.com. March 23, 2016. Accessed May 29, 2020. https://www.biography.com/writer/jose-marti.

Kamin, Blair. "1927 Athletic Club Proves Fit for Luxury Apartments." *Chicago Tribune*. March 07, 2014. Accessed October 9, 2020. https://www.chicagotribune.com/news/ct-xpm-2014-03-07-ct-met-athleticclub-20140307-story.html.

Karlson, Norman. *American Art Tile: 1876–1941*. New York: Rizzoli, 1998.

"Kennan Building—Dan Duckham Architect: Organic Architectural Design Services," Dan Duckham Architect | Organic Architectural Design Services, 1991. Accessed March 16, 2019, http://www.danduckham.com/kennan-building

Kovel, Ralph M., and Terry H. Kovel. *Kovels' American Art Pottery*. New York: Crown Publishers, 1993.

_____. *The Kovels' Collectors Guide to American Art Pottery*. New York: Crown, 1974.

Lage, Chad. *Pictorial Guide to Pottery & Porcelain Marks*. Paducah, KY: Collector Books, 2004.

"Land Reutilization Corporation." Muskingum County, Ohio. 2020. Accessed May 14, 2020. https://www.muskingumcountyoh.gov/Muskingum-County-Land-Reutilization-Corporation/.

"Landing of Columbus." Architect of the Capitol. Accessed October 31, 2020. https://www.aoc.gov/explore-capitol-campus/art/landing-columbus.

Langenbeck, Karl, and Herman C. Mueller. Tile-Setting. US Patent 664,169, filed July 13, 1900, and issued December 18, 1900.

"Late 1920's Original and Intact Polychromatic Lakeshore Drive Athletic Club Glazed Red Clay Interior Pool Room Figural 'Clam Shell' Wall Tile." Urban Remains. Accessed January 7, 2019. https://www.urbanremainschicago.com/late-1920-s-original-and-intact-polychromatic-lakeshore-drive-athletic-club-glazed-red-clay-interior-pool-room-figural-clam-shell-wall-tile.html.

"Legion Starts New Home Building Fund Selling Local Tile." *The Times Recorder* (Zanesville), August 20, 1929." Accessed May 30, 2020.

Lehner, Lois. *Ohio Pottery and Glass: Marks and Manufacturers*. Des Moines, IA: Wallace-Homestead Book, 1978.

"Lenhart Mansion Walls Are Found during Renovation of Apartments." *The Times Recorder* (Zanesville), December 10, 1990. Accessed February 21, 2019.

Lewis, Thomas W. "History of Zanesville and Muskingum County." *The Times Recorder* (Zanesville), September 27, 1924. Accessed November 10, 2019.

"Long-Term Assessment Monitoring Mosaic Tile Dump." Kevin O'Hara to Brad Stimple. October 22, 2019. U.S. EPA Region 5, Westlake, Ohio.

Lynch, Kathryn, and Michael S. Sims. *Zanesville*. Charleston, SC: Arcadia, 2005.

MacDonald, Gene L. "Former Tile Properties Utilized." *The Times Recorder* (Zanesville), April 25, 1972. Accessed March 24, 2019.

Macdonald, Herbert G., David J. Barbour, and Karl M. Claus. Multiple Unit Ceramic Tile Assembly. US Patent US3041785A, filed January 9, 1959, and issued July 3, 1962.

Macdonald, Herbert G., David J. Barbour, Karl M. Claus, and Robert B. Cleverly. Method of Fabricating a Multiple Unit Assembly. US Patent 3,185,748, filed January 27, 1961, and issued May 25, 1965.

"March 23–27, 1913: Statewide Flood." Accessed September 19, 2020. http://ohsweb.ohiohistory.org/swio/pages/content/1913_flood.htm.

Martin, Chuck. "Gene Griffin Was a Record-Setting Flyer." *The Times Recorder* (Zanesville), October 21, 1995. Accessed November 14, 2019.

_____. "A Look at Muskingum County's History." *The Times Recorder* (Zanesville), February 21, 2005. Accessed August 18, 2020.

_____. "S.S. *Zanesville* Launched with Great Fanfare." *The Times Recorder* (Zanesville), January 26, 2002. Accessed October 10, 2020.

"Materials Used in Auditorium Reach Astronomical Figures." *The Times Recorder* (Zanesville), April 15, 1940. Accessed January 12, 2019.

Matthews, Peggy. "Historic Garfield Razed, but Memories Linger on." *The Times Recorder* (Zanesville), April 17, 2001. Accessed October 3, 2020.

_____. "Lead Danger Is Found Here." *The Times Recorder* (Zanesville), August 16, 1991. Accessed May 16, 2020.

"Matthews House." n.d. Muskingum County History. Accessed October 24, 2020. http://www.muskingumcountyhistory.org/matthews-house-1.

"Modern Store Building Is Penney's Pre-Christmas Gift to Zanesville." *The Times Recorder* (Zanesville), November 4, 1953. Accessed May 17, 2019.

"Mosaic Has Hobby Package." *The Times Recorder* (Zanesville), April 26, 1958. Accessed May 31, 2020.

"Mosaic Identifies Takeover Leaders." *The Times Recorder* (Zanesville), February 22, 1967. Accessed September 20, 2020.

"Mosaic Opens New Warehouse in Tennessee." *The Times Recorder* (Zanesville), October 17, 1960. Accessed September 27, 2020.

"Mosaic Products on Luxury Liner America." *The Times Recorder* (Zanesville), January 5, 1940. Accessed May 19, 2019.

"Mosaic Reaffirms Plant Closing." *The Times Recorder* (Zanesville), March 24, 1967. Accessed January 28, 2019.

"Mosaic Tile." *The Times Recorder* (Zanesville), November 27, 1899. Accessed August 30, 2020.

"Mosaic Tile ... Now on Duty in New Good Samaritan Hospital Addition, Too." *The Times Recorder* (Zanesville), December 12, 1956. Accessed March 24, 2019.

"Mosaic Tile Co. Is Largest Firm of Its Kind in Country." *The Times Recorder,* October 2, 1947. Accessed March 22, 2019.

Mosaic Tile Company. *Hand Book of Mosaic Clay-Tiles.* Zanesville, OH: Mosaic Tile Company, 1939.

_____. *Mosaic Tile Catalog.* Ironton, OH: Mosaic Tile Company, 1938.

Mosaic Tile Company 1894–1944: Fiftieth Anniversary Program. Zanesville, OH: Mosaic Tile Company, 1944.

"Mosaic Tile Company Records: Collection Synopsis." Accessed December 28, 2018. https://www.ohiomemory.org/digital/collection/aids/id/6080.

"The Mosaic Tile Company's Works." *Brick & Clayworker* VI, no. 3 (March 1897).

"Mosaic Tile Dumpsite Focus of Cleanup." *American Recycler.* May 2003. Accessed December 25, 2018. http://www.americanrecycler.com/may2003/mosaic.html.

"Mosaic Tile Promotes Two Executives Here." *The Times Recorder* (Zanesville), August 11, 1962. Accessed September 27, 2020.

"Mosaic Tile Ready to Meet Expected Boom in Building." *The Times Recorder* (Zanesville), June 22, 1957. Accessed March 24, 2019.

"Mosaic Tile to Close Pershing Road Plant." *The Times Recorder* (Zanesville), October 28, 1966. Accessed February 5, 2019.

Mueller, Herman C. "Ceramic Mosaic." *The Clay-Worker* XXXIX, no. 1 (January 1903).

_____. Process of and Apparatus for Manufacturing Mosaics. US Patent 537,703, filed April 12, 1894, and issued April 16, 1895.

"Mural for Conservancing [*sic*] District." *The Times Recorder* (Zanesville), June 3, 1958. Accessed October 8, 2020.

Murphy, James L. *James L. Murphy's Checklist of 19th-Century Bluebird Potters and Potteries in Muskingum County, Ohio.* Edited by Jeff Carskadden and Richard Gartley. Zanesville, OH: Muskingum Valley Archaeological Survey, 2014.

Murphy, James L., and James F. Morton. *Muskingum Bluebirds: A Preliminary Checklist of Nineteenth Century Potters and Potteries in Muskingum County, Ohio.* Columbus, Ohio, 1986: 103–111.

Muskingum County. Auditor. Property Data. Zanesville, OH, 2020. Parcel 81–65–02–09–000

_____. Tax Data. Zanesville, OH, 2018. Parcel 82–27–01–04–000

Muskingum County. Recorder's Office. Assignment and Assumption Agreement. Vol. 10. Page 188. April 1977

_____. Grant Index to Deeds—Muskingum County, Ohio—Grantors. Record Vol. 596. Page 103. August 1971.

_____. Limited Warranty Deed. Book 1778. Page 181. June 2003.

_____. *Online Land Records.* Zanesville, OH, 2003–2017.

_____. Satisfaction of Mortgage. 194th ed. Vol. 945. September 1986.

"Muskingum County GIS." Muskingum County Auditor. Accessed December 26, 2018. http://www.muskingumcountyauditor.org.

"Muskingum County History Timeline." *The Times Recorder* (Zanesville), February 21, 2005. Accessed August 18, 2020.

"Muskingum River." Muskingum River—Ohio History Central. Accessed March 9, 2019. http://ohiohistorycentral.org/w/Muskingum_River.

Muskingum Watershed Conservancy District. "Great Flood of 1913 Led to MWCD, System of Dams and Reservoirs." March 24, 2013. Accessed January 18, 2019. https://www.mwcd.org/news/2013/03/24/great-flood-of-1913-led-to-mwcd-system-of-dams-and-reservoirs.

Mussi, Susan. "Ceramic—Pottery Dictionary." Accessed August 16, 2020. http://ceramicdictionary.com/en/m/414/mill.

Myroth, Greg. "Ohio Art Pottery." *Art Pottery Blog*, June 9, 2008. Accessed February 19, 2020. artpotteryblog.com/site/2008/06/ohio-art-potter.html.

"National Building Museum––Washington, D.C." MDT Travels. Accessed March 14, 2019. https://www.moderndaytripper.com/national-building-museum-washington-dc/.

"New Idea in Recreation—All-Tile, Outdoor Shuffleboard!" *The Mountain Echo* (Shickshinny, PA), March 9, 1951. Accessed January 28, 2019.

"The New Jersey Mosaic Tile Co., Matawan, N.J." *Brick XIX*, no. 3 (September 1, 1903).

"Ohio Ceramic Center Described in Historical Society Bulletin." *The Times Recorder* (Zanesville), February 14, 1971. Accessed April 5, 2020.

Ohio Historic Places Dictionary. Vol. 2. St. Clair, MI: Somerset Publishers, 1999.

"Ohio Soft Drink Bottling Plants." RoadsideArchitecture.com. Accessed January 7, 2019. https://www.roadarch.com/beverage/oh.html.

"Old Roseville Pottery Property to Be Sold at Auction June 27." *The Times Recorder* (Zanesville), June 12, 1968. Accessed March 24, 2019.

"Pace-Setter Home Theme of Talk." *The Times Recorder* (Zanesville), May 8, 1951. Accessed September 23, 2020.

"Pace-Setter House for 1951." *Tampa Bay Times* (St. Petersburg), September 9, 1951. Accessed September 23, 2020.

Padwee, Michael. "Architectural Tiles, Glass and Ornamentation In New York." December 1, 2016. Accessed April 2, 2020. https://tilesinnewyork.blogspot.com/2016.

_____. "Tile Back Views." *Flash Point*, January/June 1993.

"Part of a Ceramic-tile Mural by Works Project Administration Artist Kenneth Gale, Depicting Texas History, at the Will Rogers Auditorium, Now Part of the Will Rogers Memorial Center in Fort Worth, Texas." The Library of Congress. October 2012. Accessed May 7, 2020. https://www.loc.gov/item/2013650766.

Peck, Herbert. *The Book of Rookwood Pottery*. Cincinnati, OH: Crown Publishing Group, 1968.

"Penney's Salutes Mosaic Tile!" *The Times Recorder* (Zanesville), October 6, 1960. Accessed December 26, 2019.

"Peoples Savings Bank Will Keep Open House Two Days." *The Times Recorder* (Zanesville), August 4, 1926. Accessed February 24, 2019.

Perry, Barbara A. *American Art Pottery from the Collection of Everson Museum of Art*. New York: Harry N. Abrams, 1997.

Pinkard, Cliff. "Researchers Trying to Put Flood of 1913 Back in Public's Consciousness on Its 100th Anniversary." Cleveland.com. March 22, 2013. Accessed November 18, 2019. Cleveland.com/metro/index.ssf/2013/03/researchers_trying_to_put_floo.html.

"Political Tiles from the Mosaic Tile Co., Zanesville, Ohio, Group of 7, Including Washington, Franklin, Lincoln, & More." Cowan's Auction House. Accessed April 2, 2020. https://www.cowanauctions.com/lot/political-tiles-from-the-mosaic-tile-co-zanesville-ohio-group-of-7-including-washington-franklin-lincoln-more-173240.

"The Potteries of Zanesville, Ohio." *The Clay-Worker* XXXVII, no. 6 (June 1902). Accessed January 1, 2019.

Pratt, Kathie. "Profiles: Of People and the Times." *The Times Recorder* (Zanesville), May 12, 1968. Accessed November 27, 2019.

"Purchased Main Street Shop." *The Times Recorder* (Zanesville), December 3, 1949. Accessed October 7, 2020.

Purviance, Evan, and Louise Purviance. *Zanesville Art Tile in Color*. Des Moines, IA: Wallace-Homestead Book, 1972.

"Putnam and Zanesville: The Story of Two Cities." *Exploring the Ycity*, 18 Sept. 2013, exploringycity.wordpress.com/2013/09/19/putnam-and-zanesville-the-story-of-two-cities/.

"Question: When Is a Door Not a Door?" *The Times Recorder* (Zanesville), June 4, 1955. Accessed March 22, 2019.

Rickett, Beth. "Fourth Street Building Houses Many Different Businesses over the Years." *The Times Recorder* (Zanesville), August 13, 1990. Accessed February 24, 2019.

_____. "Hotel Rogge." *The Times Recorder* (Zanesville), April 9, 1990. Accessed March 22, 2019.

_____. "Memories Remain Though Schools Are Gone." *The Times Recorder* (Zanesville), April 23, 1990. Accessed October 3, 2020.

Ries, Heinrich, and Henry Leighton. *History of the Clay-working Industry in the United States*. 1st ed. New York: John Wiley & Sons, 1909.

"Rosario, Argentina." Encyclopædia Britannica. Accessed October 11, 2020. https://www.britannica.com/place/Rosario-Argentina.

"Rotarians to Hear Well Known Artist." *The Zanesville Signal*, March 28, 1938. Accessed November 17, 2020.

"Rotary Reporter: Shuffleboard Is a Teen-age Hit." *The Rotarian*, January 1951.

Rudloff, Jim. "Department Store Nears End of Its Era." *The Times Recorder* (Zanesville), February 6, 1997. Accessed October 5, 2020.

Rumer, Anna. "Bloomer Candy Production Moves." *The Times Recorder* (Zanesville), May 21, 2014. Accessed October 4, 2020.

"S.S. *Zanesville*." *The Times Recorder* (Zanesville), December 8, 1944. Accessed August 30, 2020.

"Sagger." Dictionary.com. Accessed October 31, 2020. https://www.dictionary.com/browse/sagger.

Sanders, Sharon. "The Art of Printing." SeMissourian.com. February 28, 2013. Accessed May 25, 2020. https://www.semissourian.com/blogs/fromthemorgue/entry/51580.

Sanford, Martha, and Steve Sanford. *Sanfords' Guide to Pottery by McCoy.* Campbell, CA: Adelmore Press, 1997.

Schneider, Norris F. *Bethesda, Your Hospital.* Zanesville, OH: Bethesda Hospital Association, 1965.

———. "Building Was Only 31 Years Old." *The Times Recorder* (Zanesville), January 20, 1963. Accessed February 25, 2019.

———. "Dedication of New County Home Wing to Occur Today." *The Times Recorder* (Zanesville), March 11, 1973, sec. D. Accessed October 4, 2020.

———. *The Dr. Increase Mathews House: Home of Pioneer and Historical Society of Muskingum County.* Zanesville, OH: N.p., 1975.

———. "Floor Tile Made Here Is Still in Use Nationwide." *The Times Recorder* (Zanesville), May 28, 1972. Accessed January 18, 2019.

———. *The History of South Zanesville* (Zanesville: The Times Recorder, 1957), quoted in *South Zanesville, OH, Centennial 1890–1990, Souvenir Book.* Zanesville, OH: N.p., 1990.

———. *History of Zanesville High School.* Zanesville, OH: Creative Graphics of Ohio, 1988.

———. "Karl Langenbeck Helped Establish Mosaic Tile." *The Times Recorder* (Zanesville), March 8, 1970. Accessed April 16, 2020.

———. *The McIntire Estate: 1815–1980.* Zanesville, OH: Zanesville Canal and Manufacturing, 1981.

———. "Mosaic, Largest U.S. Tile Plant, Prepares to Observe 50th Birthday." *Sunday Times Signal* (Zanesville), September 10, 1944. Accessed September 13, 2020.

———. *The Muskingum River: A History and Guide.* Columbus, OH: Ohio Historical Society, 1968.

———. "Penney Closing Ends Era in Downtown Zanesville." *The Times Recorder* (Zanesville), November 2, 1980. Accessed October 3, 2020.

———. "Scholarship Funds Available for Students Here." *The Times Recorder* (Zanesville), April 1, 1973. Accessed March 24, 2019.

———. "Second Campaign for $500,000 Is Needed to Complete Construction of YMCA Here." *The Times Recorder* (Zanesville), April 16, 1961. Accessed May 20, 2020.

———. "Tile Mural in New Auditorium Symbolizes Growth of City." *The Zanesville Daily,* May 19, 1940. Accessed January 2019.

———. *Y-Bridge City: The Story of Zanesville and Muskingum County, Ohio.* Cleveland, OH: World Publishing Company, 1950.

———. *Zanesville Art Pottery.* Zanesville, OH: N.p., 1963.

"Sebaugh-Basehart Wedding Today." *The Times Recorder* (Zanesville), June 28, 1911. Accessed November 2, 2020.

"A Sermon Written on the Face of the Land..." *The Times Recorder* (Zanesville), September 30, 1960. Accessed November 10, 2019.

"Sheriff's Sale of Real Estate." *The Times Recorder* (Zanesville), January 22, 2019. Accessed May 16, 2020.

Sigafoose, Dick. *American Art Pottery: Identification & Values.* 2nd ed. Paducah, KY: Collector Books, 2006.

Sims, Michael. "OH Zanesville—S.S. *Zanesville* Victory Ship Plaque." Historic U.S. Tile Installations, O-W. November 2010. Accessed October 4, 2020. https://sites.google.com/site/tileinstallationdatabasemz/oh_zanesville—s-s-zanesville-victory-ship-plaque.

———. "The Tiles of Zanesville, OH: America's Tile Manufacturing Center." *Flash Point* Vol. 6, No. 3 (July-September 1993): 19.

"629 Main St." *Times Signal* (Zanesville), March 27, 1959. Accessed October 4, 2020.

"Some Mosaic Assets Sold by Marmon." *The Times Recorder* (Zanesville), April 27, 1968. Accessed February 5, 2019.

"Souvenir Program: Dedication Noble County Court House." Ohio Memory Collection. 1934. Accessed April 26, 2020. https://ohiomemory.org/digital/collection/p267401coll36/id/15488.

Specifications of the Materials and Labor to Be Used and Employed in the Erection of First Evangelical United Brethren Church. Cambridge, OH: Sigman & Tribbie, Registered Architects, 1959.

Starbuck, Barbara J. "Mission Possible: Preservationists Want to Turn Garfield into Museum, Community Gathering Place." *The Times Recorder* (Zanesville), December 10, 1991. Accessed October 3, 2020.

"State Capitol—Eureka Tiles." California State Capitol Museum in Sacramento, California. Accessed April 17, 2020. http://capitolmuseum.ca.gov/architecture-and-history/architectural-virtual-tour.

State of Ohio. Seventy-Second General Assembly. *Annual Reports for 1895.* Columbus, OH: Westbote Co., 1896.

Stimple, Brad. *Mosaic Tile Dump Site Operable Unit (OU) 1.* EPA OSC Response. Zanesville, OH: Ohio Environmental Protection Agency, 2020.

Stokes, Sally Sims. "Documenting the History of the White House Library Fireplace Tiles, 1944–1962." *Art Documentation: Journal of the Art Libraries Society of North America* 36, no. 1 (2017): 50–72. Accessed January 18, 2020. doi:10.1086/691372.

"The Story of the S.S. *America.*" Sometimes Interesting. June 27, 2011. Accessed May 25, 2020. https://sometimes-interesting.com/2011/06/27/the-ss-america/.

Strazzabosco, Peter. "Union Park Hotel Approved for Landmark Status." June 9, 2010. Accessed May 25, 2020. https://www.chicago.gov/city/en/depts/dcd/provdrs/hist/news/2010/mar/union_park_hotelproposedforlandmarkstatus.html.

Summer 2013 Groundwater Monitoring Report. Project no. 21–18216A. United States Environmental Protection Agency, Region 5 and Ohio

Environmental Protection Agency. Chicago, IL: ENVIRON International Corporation, 2013.

Sutor, J. Hope. *Past and Present of the City of Zanesville and Muskingum County, Ohio.* Chicago: S.J. Clarke Publishing Company, 1905.

"Swimming Pool Opened at Country Club." *The Times Recorder* (Zanesville), August 31, 1953. Accessed February 1, 2019.

Taft, Lisa Factor. "Herman Carl Mueller (1854–1941), Innovator in the Field of Architectural Ceramics" (PhD diss. Ohio State University, 1979), https://etd.ohiolink.edu/pg_10?0::NO:1 0:P10_ACCESSION_NUM:osu1487084652613915

"Taylor Gets Contract for New Building." *The Times Recorder* (Zanesville), February 12, 1959. Accessed May 20, 2020.

Taylor-Lehman, Dylan. "The Ups and Downs of Being a Canal Lockmaster." *Atlas Obscura.* August 15, 2018. Accessed March 9, 2019. https://www.atlasobscura.com/articles/river-canal-lock-master.

"This Morning's Paper Printed at New Plant." *The Times Recorder* (Zanesville), September 27, 1926. Accessed February 24, 2019.

"3-Day ZTC Starts Today." *The Times Recorder* (Zanesville), June 16, 1978. Accessed November 27, 2019.

"Tile and Mantel Dealers to Meet." *The Buffalo Commercial,* January 24, 1916. Accessed October 11, 2020.

"Tile Firm Acquired by Stylon." *The Morning Call* (Allentown), May 5, 1968. Accessed September 20, 2020.

"Tile Mural Unveiled on New Building." *The Times Recorder* (Zanesville), October 3, 1958. Accessed February 24, 2019.

Tile Terms Glossary. Accessed September 22, 2020. https://www.tilemountain.co.uk/tile_terms_glossary.

Titusville Historic Walking Tour. PDF. Titusville. https://visitcrawford.org/wp-content/uploads/2019/01/HIstoric-Titusville-Walking-Tour-2014-compressed.pdf

"To Break Ground for Swim Pool." *The Times Recorder* (Zanesville), May 25, 1953. Accessed January 31, 2019.

"To Combine the City Hall with Market House." *The Times Recorder* (Zanesville), February 10, 1914. Accessed February 25, 2019.

"Traffic and Transportation." *Electric Railway Journal,* April 2, 1910, 641. Accessed November 2, 2020.

2015 Groundwater Monitoring Report. Project no. 21–18216A. United States Environmental Protection Agency, Region 5 and Ohio Environmental Protection Agency. Chicago: Ramboll Environ, 2017.

United States Tariff Commission. *Tariff Commission Reports to the President on Ceramic Mosaic Tile Workers' Petition for Adjustment Assistance.* Washington, D.C., 1963.

"U.S. Engineer Office." *Marietta Daily Leader*, April 6, 1899. Accessed March 9, 2019.

"Use Mosaic Tile in New Building." *The Times Recorder* (Zanesville), May 19, 1955. Accessed May 17, 2019.

VAP Phase I Property Assessment. Report. Ohio: SME, 2017. Project Number 074522.00.04A.002 Senior Consultant Keith B. Egan.

"Walleisa Has Fabrics from Pace-setter House by 'House Beautiful.'" *Pottsville Republican*, May 3, 1951. Accessed September 23, 2020.

Ward, Betty Purviance, and Nancy N. Schiffer. *Weller, Roseville & Related Zanesville Art Pottery & Tiles.* Atglen, PA: Schiffer Publishing, 2000.

"We Congratulate." *The Times Recorder* (Zanesville), June 12, 1954. Accessed May 17, 2019.

"What Is the Difference between Overglaze and Underglaze?" DPH Trading. Accessed September 22, 2020. https://www.dphtrading.com/customer-service/guides/tips-and-ideas/what-is-the-difference-between-overglaze-und-underglaze#:~text=in the case of.

"Will Rogers Memorial Center's Coliseum and Auditorium Tile Murals." Fort Worth Public Art. Accessed May 7, 2020. https://fwpublicart.org/will-rogers/.

"William M. Shinnick Educational Fund." William M. Shinnick Educational Fund. Accessed March 4, 2020. https://www.shinnickeducationalfund.com/About-William-M-Shinnick-Educational-Fund-Muskingum-County-Ohio/.

"Williams Delicatessen." *The Times Recorder* (Zanesville), October 2, 1947. Accessed February 12, 2019.

Wires, E. Stanley, Norris F. Schneider, and Moses Mesre. *Zanesville Decorative Tiles.* Zanesville, OH: N.p., 1972.

"Y Bridge." n.d. Visit Zanesville Muskingum County Ohio. Muskingum County Convention Visitors Bureau. Accessed January 28, 2019. http://www.visitzanesville.com/Explore/Destinations/175/Y-Bridge/#.

Zanesville Official City Directory and Complete Classified Business and Professional Directory. Akron, OH: Burch Directory Company, 1939.

Zanesville Official City Directory and Complete Classified Business and Professional Directory, 1910. Akron, OH: Burch Directory, 1909.

_____, 1924. Akron, OH: Burch Directory Company, 1923.

_____, 1926–27. Akron, OH: Burch Directory Company, 1926.

_____, 1928–29. Akron, OH: Burch Directory Company, 1928.

"Zanesville, Ohio." n.d. Zanesville, Ohio—Ohio History Central. Accessed September 6, 2020. https://ohiohistorycentral.org/w/Zanesville,_Ohio.

Index

Numbers in **_bold italics_** indicate pages with illustrations